**Disclaimer:** This book is for general informational and educational purposes only and is not a substitute for professional advice. The author accepts no responsibility for any loss, damage, or injury (including emotional or psychological) that may arise from the use of this material. If you or your child are experiencing bullying, grooming, exploitation, mental health issues, or any crisis, please seek immediate help from a qualified professional or the services listed inside this book.

Some statistics, facts, and guidelines are adapted from publicly available materials from the eSafety Commissioner and other Australian government sources. These materials are used in accordance with their licensing terms and, where applicable, are licensed under CC BY 4.0.

This book contains affiliate links. The author may receive a small commission at no extra cost to you if you purchase through these links. All trademarks, product names, and brand names belong to their respective owners and are used for reference purposes only.

This book was created with basic assistance from Grok, an AI developed by xAI. The author provided all research, personal stories, direction, editing, and final approval of every page.

ISBN: 978-1-7641309-4-3
First published in Australia, 2026.

This book discusses real online risks including bullying, grooming, exploitation, and the difficult situation when a child is the one causing harm. Some sections may be emotionally challenging. If you or your family are currently experiencing any of these issues, please reach out to the support services listed on Pages 51, 81 or contact a professional immediately.

# Welcome to the no-nonsense Guide

Dear Parents,

Welcome to the no-nonsense guide to online safety.
A book designed to take the stress and complexity away from learning the ins and outs of the internet by stripping everything back with an easy-to-follow guide to get you up to date with how fast technology is moving.

It's a scary time for us, especially if you're in the category of being last generation to grow up without social media or the internet dominating everything as it does today. And you might think, "Oh, it won't happen to me"... but trust me, from personal experience that I'll go over on the next page, it could end up being a lot closer than you think.

When designing the book, I set out with the simple overall mission to help families navigate the internet in a safe but fun way, putting the power back into parents' hands, while building trust and knowledge that might be new or even overwhelming to some.
Let's walk through it together.

**Nathan Martin**
Concerned Uncle, One day Parent

# Why Do This?

I've always been known as the techy uncle, the one who gets excited about every new gadget and loves staying ahead of where technology is heading.

But when my niece and nephew came along, I started to worry. I watched them grow up in the iPad era of parenting, devices handed over to keep them quiet. And yes, I did benefit from those "quiet times," so I didn't push as hard as I should have.

Then one day it all changed. My 10-year-old niece was being bullied online by someone we thought was her friend. When we were shown the messages telling her to kill herself, it absolutely broke our hearts. The secret texting, the anger when anyone touched her phone, it all suddenly made sense.

Seeing my sister feel completely powerless and lost in that moment killed me. But it didn't stop there.

While checking my 6-year-old nephew's devices, we discovered TikTok and Roblox accounts where grown men were adding him because his profile wasn't private. He was playing scary games at night and struggling to sleep. It was terrifying. Of course, when my sister tried to research online, she was flooded with hundreds of articles of "do this, do that" guides, and honestly at that point she gave up.

That was the moment I stepped in. I started setting up their devices properly, adding protections, and helping my sister reset their family's whole approach to online safety.

It wasn't until I began doing all this that I started to ask the question: "Why hasn't anyone made a simple, dumbed-down guide that's just easy for busy parents?" That's when the vision for this book became clear.

And yes, I don't have a degree. I'm not as smart as the professionals online, and they are definitely who you should reach out to for serious concerns. But for me, I couldn't just sit there complaining on Facebook. I saw something that hurt my family and decided to build a tool to help other parents avoid that same pain.

Chances are, you're reading this right now as a parent who feels overwhelmed, worried, or even a little scared about keeping your kids safe online. I'll do my best to change that for you. But as a warning: I tried to cover everything, so some Sections, like the one about when your own child might be the bully, might feel uncomfortable. But they're there because they need to be spoken about.

The digital world moves so fast. New apps, new risks, new fears every single week. One minute you're trying to figure out parental controls; the next you're lying awake wondering if you're doing enough or if you're already falling behind.

The mission of this book is simple: putting the power back in parents' hands all around Australia, so you can feel safe online again.

You're not alone in this. You've already taken the first brave step by picking up this book.

So why keep talking about it? Let's go!!!

# Table Of Contents

Don't feel overwhelmed; you can read it all or just what you need to know now!


Pages 9–16

**The Digital Jungle: Why Online Safety Matters**

Kick off with eye-opening stats, a quick parent quiz, and a simple family audit to help you understand the real risks, without the scare tactics.

Pages 17–28

**Setting Up Camp: Device Basics and Parental Controls**

Hands-on step-by-step guides for iOS and Android, recommended tools, troubleshooting tips, and quick challenges to lock down devices fast.

Pages 29–36

**Modelling the Way: Be the Digital Role Model Your Kids Need**

Self-reflection quiz, practical family rules and zones, and a ready-to-use media agreement to help you lead by example every day.

Pages 37–46

**Talking the Talk: Having Those Awkward Chats**

Age-specific scripts, role-play scenarios, warning signs checklist, and a chat tracker to make those important conversations easier and more effective.

Pages 47–52

**Spotting the Snakes: Recognise and Handle Cyberbullying**

Types of bullying, empathy-building exercises, clear reporting steps to eSafety, and support tools to help your child bounce back strong.

# Table Of Contents

Don't feel overwhelmed; you can read it all or just what you need to know now!


**When the Snake is in Your Own Nest: If Your Child is Bullying Others** — Pages53-64

Compassionate, shame-free guidance on handling the shock and guilt, having honest conversations, applying accountability, and preventing it from happening again.

**Privacy Pirates: Protecting Personal Info and Avoiding Scams** — Pages 65-74

Password and 2FA basics, scam spotter game, app settings guide, and family privacy pledge to keep your information safe from digital thieves.

**The Dark Side: Dealing with Exploitation and Inappropriate Content** — Pages 75-82

Red flags and real scenarios, reporting and recovery steps, and trusted professional resources to handle the toughest situations with confidence.

**Levelling Up: Ongoing Strategies and Resources** — Pages 83-98

Monthly check-ins, 30-day challenge calendar, full resource directory, and a victory lap quiz to keep your family's safety strong long-term.

**You've Got This: Your Family's Safe Future Starts Now** — Pages 99-118

Celebrate everything you've learned, create your own family safety plan, and finish with real motivation and next steps, Safety Signal Cards explanation as well as additional resources for you to use, plus a notes section if you need it.

Almost 3 in 4 Aussie kids (74%) have seen or heard harmful content online; let's change that together!

# The Digital Jungle: Why Online Safety Matters

G'day, parents! Let's kick things off by comparing the internet to a wild Aussie bushwalk, full of exciting discoveries, but with a few hidden snakes and prickly bits.

As a parent in Australia (or anywhere that's not Down Under), you might feel like you're navigating it blindfolded. But here's the good news: You're not alone, and it's not as scary as it seems. This section kicks off our guide by showing why online safety matters, without overwhelming you with doom and gloom.

We'll chuck in some eye-opening facts, a quick quiz to see where you stand, and easy tools to get started. Think of it as your first step to becoming the family hero! So pick up your shield in hand, and get ready to tackle the digital wilds.

Let's face it, the online world moves fast. But realising the risks doesn't mean locking away the devices; it's about smart, balanced habits. Recent stats from the eSafety Commissioner show that while kids love the web for fun and learning, it's got a dodgy side too. With over half (53%) of Aussie children facing cyberbullying, and 60% having seen online hate already, the worry for parents is real!

Many feel under-equipped, but simple steps can make a huge difference. Over the course of the book, I'll be casting a large net over as many common subjects that I believe are essential for parents to know now, and I'll probably sound like a broken record by the end of this, but hopefully in doing so I help you in some way.

If you learn anything from this book, always remember it's not about being the "fun police"; with rules and regulations, it's about guiding your kids to be tech-savvy explorers.

## Key Stats to Wake You Up (Without the Panic)

74% of children have encountered harmful content online, things like violence or misinformation that can stick in young minds.

Cyberbullying hits 53% of kids, often through apps or games, with mean messages causing more emotional pain than stubbing your toe.

1 in 4 (25%) face non-consensual tracking or harassment, which is creepy stuff, but luckily for us it's reportable to the eSafety website.

On the bright side, 96% of 10-15-year-olds use social media for connection, so there is some good in connecting with friends.

# Common Risks Breakdown

In the digital jungle, there are a few critters to be aware of, but recognising them early can make a big difference. Here's a straightforward breakdown serious enough to start taking action today! We'll look at full breakdowns later on.

**Cyberbullying:**

Mean messages or exclusion that sting like a bluebottle jellyfish. It affects 53% of kids, often on social media.

Signs: Your child seems withdrawn after screen time.

**Grooming and Exploitation:**

Strangers building "friendships" to trick kids.
Red flag if they're secretive about chats.

14% of 10-15-year-olds report grooming behaviours.

**Harmful Content:**

Exposure to violence, hate, or misinformation
74% of kids have seen it.

Like junk food for the brain, filters help.

**Oversharing and Privacy Risks:**

Kids posting too much, leading to scams or tracking.
25% experience harassment.

"The web's not the enemy; it's just a playground with some rough patches. Let's add safety nets!

# Parent Quiz: How Tech Savvy Are You?

Time for a bit of fun! Do your best and try to answer honestly. This quick quiz (5 questions) helps you realise your starting point. No judgement, even tech pros slip up!

**1.** Do you know your child's top three used apps or sites?
YES NO

**2.** Can you spot a phishing scam?
YES NO

**3.** Have you set up parental controls on their devices?
YES NO

**4.** Do you model good habits, like no phones at dinner?
YES NO

**5.** Do you chat regularly about online strangers or sharing pics?
YES NO

| | Tally Your Yeses! |
|---|---|
| 5 Yeses: | **You're a Digital Guru**<br>top job, keep leading the way! |
| 3-4 Yeses: | **Solid Explorer**<br>on track, but let's boost those weak spots. |
| 1-2 Yeses: | **Bush Beginner**<br>No worries, this guide's your map to mastery. |
| 0 Yeses: | **Digital Newbie**<br>Welcome aboard; small changes start here! |

# Family Audit Checklist: Quick Self-Assessment Tool

Alright, let's get hands-on. This 5-minute audit helps you spot gaps without the fuss. Fill in as you go; help is below. It's like a home safety check, but for screens!
(Extra page Audit's Page 105)

| App | Risk | Screen Time | Ask the Child What have they seen lately? (Apps, Videos, Posts, etc.) |
|---|---|---|---|
| | | | |
| | | | |
| | | | |
| | | | |

## Pro Tips

This is just a basic tool to check apps already installed on kids' devices, but don't worry, we will go over everything in later parts, such as finding and setting up screen time, etc.

1. **Devices**
   List the apps on your child's phone, tablet, TV or laptop

2. **Risk**
   Full Risk dive on the next page if stuck, rate each 1-5 for privacy/sharing risks. Note fixes: E.g., "Instagram: 4, public profile; switch to private."

3. **Screen Time**
   Rate 1-5 (under 2 hours daily = low, over = high). Note habits: E.g., "Evenings spike to 3 hours."

4. **Ask your child: "Have you seen anything weird or upsetting online lately?"**
   Rate their response 1-5 for concern level. Note details: E.g., scary video, violent post, etc.

**Repeat monthly! If ratings average over 3, quick fixes covered next.**

# Deeper Dive on Risks

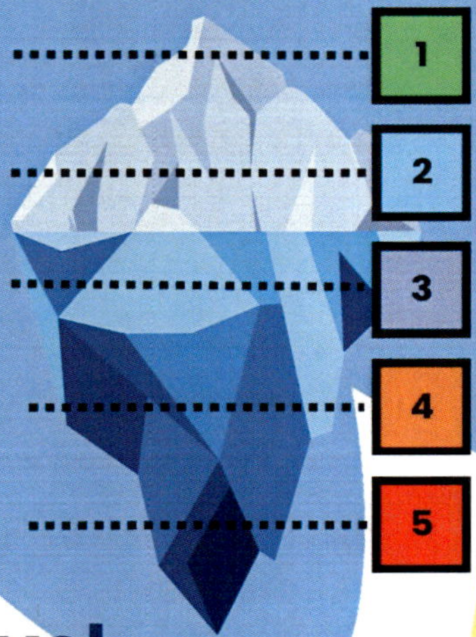


Not to dwell on the dark stuff but understanding helps you rate smarter. We've expanded the common risks from earlier with a 1-5 scale. Why harsh ratings? Because even low risks can escalate if ignored (e.g., a fun app turns dodgy with bad behaviour). Use this to prioritise blue for chill, red for action. (No one's suggesting you bin the iPad!).

# So Why Rate So Harshly? Quick Reasons by Risk Level

Here's why we go from blue to red with real examples to help you score your family's setup. Remember, it's not about perfection; it's about progress!

| | | |
|---|---|---|
| **Level 1** | **Super safe** | Educational apps like ABC Kids have no chats or ads. They feature strong filters, no sharing, and parent-approved content. There is a low harm risk, where kids learn without worries. |
| **Level 2** | **Mostly harmless** | Simple games like Minecraft in creative mode. Has Some online elements, but limited interactions, easy for parental oversight keeping it chill. |
| **Level 3** | **Watchable** | YouTube Kids with ads. With the Potential for odd videos slipping through; it needs filters, but not a full panic (53% of kids see mild junk here). |
| **Level 4** | **Risky business** | Social apps like Snapchat with disappearing messages. Have a high chance of oversharing or bullying (25% harassment cases), where strangers can creep in, so it's time for strict rules. |
| **Level 5** | **Dodgy territory** | Unmonitored Discord servers or random chat rooms. Where Grooming risks (14% affected), harmful content floods (74% exposure), immediate blocks or talks are needed, report to eSafety pronto. |

**Rate harsh to stay sharp. You've got the tools now!**

# You've Got This: Level Up Your Family's Online Game

Hey, pat yourself on the back! In this wild digital era, you're not just surviving; you're thriving by grabbing the reins early. Think of it as upgrading from the first car you learned how to drive in, to the first time you brought a brand-new car. Smoother, safer, and way more fun. With these facts and tools, you're ditching the fear for fierce confidence by turning potential pitfalls into teachable moments. Remember, 96% of kids already navigate the web positively; you're just adding that extra shield. So, breathe easy, stay trendy with regular check-ins, and watch your family bond over safer screens. You're the MVP, now let's lock it in and keep going!

> **You're the gatekeeper, not the fun police. Let's make the web work for your family, safely and stylishly."**

95% of Aussie caregivers see online safety as a big challenge, but controls cut that stress in half!

# Setting Up Camp: Device Basics and Parental Controls

Alright, time to pitch your tent in the digital outback!
If Level 1 showed why safety matters, this one's the how-to: Simple setups to lock down devices without turning into a tech tyrant or overcomplicating simple settings.
No need for a degree in IT, just follow along, and you'll have controls sorted quicker than a seatbelt heats up.

Still asking, "Why bother?"

Hands up those who brought a new device for their child only to rush through settings to hand it over as quickly as possible? It's okay, you're not alone, with a whopping 57% of Aussie parents skipping parental controls, even though 82% worry about online risks.
That leaves kids open to dodgy stuff, but not any longer. We'll cover iOS, Android, top tools, fixes, and challenges so that we can build that safe camp together!

# Quick Look

Don't worry if tech feels overwhelming; I've picked the best two apps you can use now, with steps that are straightforward and free, well, mostly. I'll cover paid apps if you are looking for that extra protection, but let's talk about parental controls. They aren't about spying; they're about guiding, like teaching road rules before handing over the car keys. In Australia, with 96% of 10-15-year-olds on social media, controls help block junk and set limits. Start with built-in tools and add apps if needed. If done right, you could reduce exposure to harms by up to 80%.

**First, let's look at common questions from parents:**

### Android or iOS?

I'm on a mission to cover all the bases, so let's make sure you're in sync with whatever kind of phone system you've got. Apple runs on the iOS platform, whereas devices such as Samsung utilise Android created by Google.

### Do parental controls really block all inappropriate content, or do I need extra filters?

Built-in tools like iOS Screen Time and Android Family Link filter content but aren't foolproof. Enhance protection with other settings covered later for better blocking. It all depends on what in particular you are having an issue with.

### Paid or Free?

First I'll show you the free options available to you right now, with settings you can change straight away. After that, I'll list a couple of paid apps that offer even more protection and control if you are looking to go the extra step. But once again, that's up to you.

### How do I set up parental controls if my kid has an iPhone but I use Android?

Use Apple's Family Sharing through iCloud.com on your Android browser or web app. Link accounts, approve apps remotely, and monitor Screen Time. For cross-platform compatibility, consider a third-party app.

### What if my child is under 13? Can they even have their own device account?

For iOS, create a child Apple ID through Family Sharing (Settings > Your Name > Family Sharing > Add Member > Create Child Account), it auto-enables restrictions.

On Android, use Google Family Link to supervise a child's Google account (no full access until 13).

This keeps things legal and safe; remember, eSafety recommends supervised accounts for under-13s to cut risks by 80%.

### How can I monitor my kid's location or activity without feeling like a spy?

iOS Family Sharing for location (Find My app) and app usage reports; Android Family Link for real-time tracking and alerts. Set it up as a family safety net, explain it's for emergencies, not snooping. This cuts worry by 50% and builds trust when discussed openly.

### Best way to limit screen time without constant battles?

Start with device defaults: iOS Downtime for scheduled blackouts, Android daily limits in Family Link. Customise by app (for example: 1 hour for games) and involve kids in setting apps; a family agreement makes it collaborative. Many parents find this reduces arguments by 60%. Track with troubleshooting bubbles if overrides happen.

### Can parental controls work on multiple devices?

Absolutely, iOS syncs via Family Sharing across Apple gear. Android Family Link links all Google devices. For mixed setups, go third-party like Qustodio (cross-platform, works seamlessly on iOS and Android). Setup tip: Link everything under one parent account for unified reports, save time, and cover 95% of family devices seamlessly.

# iOS (Apple) Step-by-Step:
## I've Got It Guide

With Screen Time, you can see how much time your child spends on their device, including which apps and websites they use the most. You can also schedule daily app limits, block content that isn't age-appropriate, and much, much more.

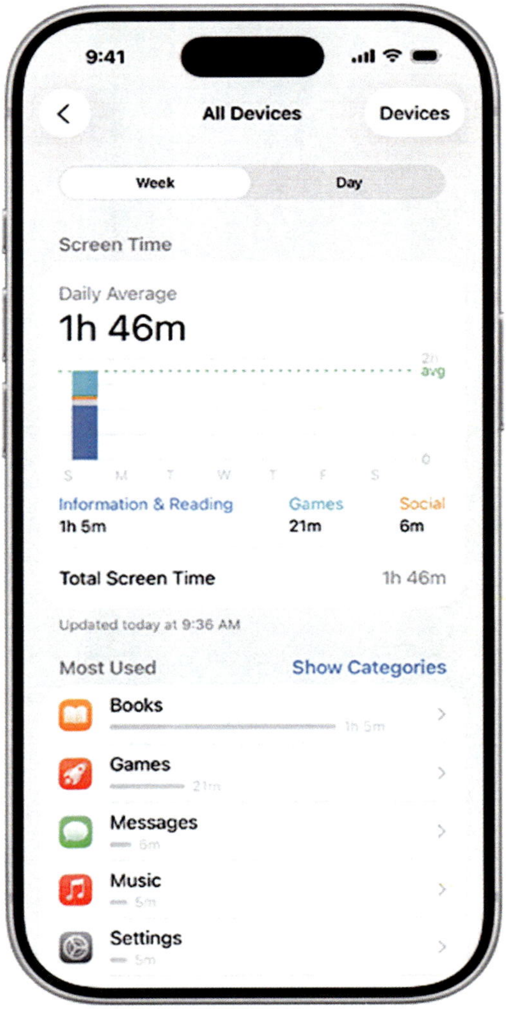


### iOS Setup

Apple's Screen Time is your mate for iPhones/iPads. Easy to set, hard to bypass (unless your kid's a hacker prodigy!). Follow these for iOS (current as of 2026).

1. Open Settings > Screen Time > Turn On Screen Time (pick "This is My Child's Device").
2. Set a passcode, something sneaky, not your birthday!
3. Tap Content & Privacy Restrictions > Enable > Set app ratings, block sites.
4. App Limits: Screen Time > App Limits > Add limits (e.g., 1 hour for TikTok).
5. Downtime: Schedule blackouts (e.g., bedtime).
6. Family Sharing: Link accounts for remote management.

# Android Step-by-Step: I've Got It Guide

Family Link from Google helps parents stay in the loop and keep their child or teen safer online as they explore across Android and ChromeOS devices.

Family Link

## Android Setup

Now for Android with Google's Family Link. A free app that syncs across devices. Download from the Play Store first.

1. Create your child's Google Account (under 13? Use Family Link to supervise).
2. Install Family Link on your phone > Add child > Link their device.
3. Set daily limits: In the app > Screen time > Daily limit (e.g., 2 hours total).
4. App approvals: Block/approve downloads; set time per app.
5. Content filters: Enable SafeSearch; block sites in Chrome.
6. Location & alerts: Track device, get low-battery notifications.

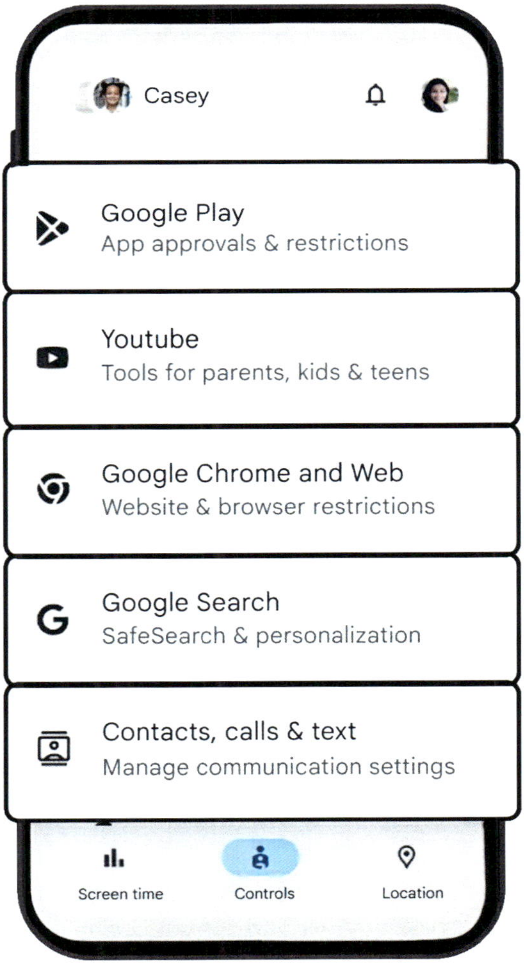


> Every parent will want something different when it comes to the levels of freedom they want their kids to have, so I've chosen these apps that consider multiple levels of restrictions and freedoms.

**If you are still struggling, both Apple and Google have an even more detailed breakdown on each website found below. Simply scan the QR code and you will be taken straight to each website.**

## Scan for Apple's Full Guide

## Google's Family Link Guide

## Extra Free Built-in Options for iOS (Apple devices)

- **Communication Safety** – Automatically detects and blurs nude or sensitive images in the Messages app before a child sees them. Parents get notified if the child tries to view or send one.
- **Family Sharing Purchase Approvals** – Every app or in-app purchase must be approved by you before it downloads , great for stopping surprise bills.
- **Focus Modes** – Set custom "Do Not Disturb" schedules that block notifications and apps during homework, dinner, or bedtime.
- **Guided Access** – Locks the child into one single app (e.g. YouTube Kids) so they can't switch to anything else.

## Extra Free Built-in Options for Android (Google devices)

- **Digital Wellbeing** – Built-in screen time dashboard, focus mode, and bedtime mode that works across all apps.
- **Google Play Protect** – Automatic daily security scans that block harmful or fake apps before they're installed.
- **SafeSearch** in Google & YouTube – Filters explicit results and videos automatically (turn it on in the Google app settings).
- **YouTube Restricted Mode** – Hides mature content in the YouTube app (free and very effective for younger kids).
- **Quick Tip** These features are all 100% free and already on the device, no downloads needed. They work really well when combined with the main controls we covered earlier.

# Troubleshooting

App Not Blocking? Update software; restart device. Remember outdated iOS misses 30% filters.

Too Restrictive? Customise per app, balance is key, or they'll rebel and test workarounds.

Kid Bypassed Controls? Change passcode weekly; use biometrics. Why? Kids are clever and you need to stay one step ahead!

Too Restrictive? Customise per app. Balance is key, or they'll rebel like a teen roo.

Alerts Overload? Tweak notifications in app settings, shifting focus to bigger risks.

You've got the basics down! Now these cross-platform gems ensure smooth sailing, whether Apple or Google. These apply to both, cutting risks by up to 80% with consistent use. No tech wizardry needed; think of them as your digital toolkit.

- **Test and Tweak Regularly:** After setup, use the device's report features (Screen Time > Insights on iOS; Family Link > Activity on Android) to review usage weekly. Why, you ask? It spots patterns like late-night scrolling and allows you to adjust.
- **Combine with Wi-Fi Controls:** Use your home router's parental settings (e.g., via an app from Telstra or Optus) to enforce house-wide rules. Why? It backs up device controls if they switch gadgets, that way we block sites at the source.
- **Enable Notifications Wisely:** Turn on alerts for limit breaches or new app requests (iOS: Screen Time > Communication; Android: Family Link > Alerts). It keeps you in the loop without spying, 57% of parents miss issues without them.
- **Age-Appropriate Customisation:** Tailor by age, stricter for under-10s (block all chats), looser for teens (time limits only). Why? It builds independence safely; you can ease restrictions as they grow. Also Use built-in ratings (iOS: Restrictions > Apps; Android: Play Store > Family) to auto-filter age-unsuitable content.
- **Backup with Education:** Pair controls with quick chats like, "Why we have limits: To keep the fun without the junk." Tools alone aren't enough; 82% of parents say talks boost effectiveness.

# Paid Apps

The free built-in tools (Apple Screen Time and Google Family Link) are great and cover the needs of most families really well. However, as kids get older and start using more apps and social media, start group chats, and play more games, some parents might find the need for a bit more help. That's where paid tools can offer extra features that the free tools don't, such as smarter alerts for bullying or grooming, easier management across multiple devices, and more detailed reports.

**When it might make sense for you**:

- Your child is on multiple devices or social media platforms
- You want early alerts about risky conversations
- You need stronger filtering or location tracking
- You're looking for simpler reports you can check quickly

**What to look out for:**

- Make sure the app works well in Australia (some features are limited here as I explain below)
- Check the privacy policy! You want a company that's transparent about what data they collect
- Start with a free trial whenever possible so you can test it with your family, all options on the next page offer exactly that.

There's no perfect solution to deciding, as the best app is the one that fits your child's age, your family's needs, and your budget.

# Why Most Apps Come from Overseas

Many of the big parental control apps are developed overseas, and there's a simple reason for that. Australia has a relatively small population, so it's hard for local companies to compete with international giants that have huge teams and big budgets.

Building a good app that works perfectly on both iOS and Android, stays up to date, and meets our strict Online Safety Act is very expensive.

The good news? Australia still has some excellent local and locally supported options that work really well for Aussie families.

# My #1 Pick

## Qustodio

by Qoria

I've been secretly testing quite a few apps while putting this book together, and Qustodio ticked the most boxes for us. It works perfectly across any phones, tablets, laptops, and even Kindles, giving you detailed screen-time reports, location tracking, and the ability to easily block apps you don't want the kids using. Setup was straightforward and simple.

What really stood out for us was the weekly reports. You can quickly switch between each child and see exactly what's happening with their different setups. The notifications are fast and clear, so you can step in right away if something concerning pops up, like a flagged unsafe link, as we experienced during our trial.

You can try Qustodio risk-free with their 30-day Premium trial.
Get Qustodio here →

## Other Options

**Boomerang**

| Android / iOS Support | Approx. Cost (AUD) | Best For |
|---|---|---|
| Yes | $60 – $90/year | Strong local support & Australian-focused features |

**Bark**

| Android / iOS Support | Approx. Cost (AUD) | Best For |
|---|---|---|
| Yes | $15 – $25 / month | Deep social media & text monitoring |

**Kaspersky Safe Kids**

| Android / iOS Support | Approx. Cost (AUD) | Best For |
|---|---|---|
| Yes | $20 – $45 / year | Best budget option |

**This is not financial advice; you should review and choose which option works best for you.**

Introduce 5-minute family huddles to build habits together. No testing limits between siblings; instead, focus on teamwork to discourage sneaky behaviour and encourage open chats. Do one a day for a week and turn it into a game with rewards, like you doing a cringy TikTok dance for them.

# Family Safety Sprint: Quick Team Activities

## 01 App Discovery

- Sit with your kid and list their devices and apps together. Discuss why each is fun/safe.
- This builds trust, allowing you to spot risks as a team without surprises.

## 02 Time Limit Chat

- Pick one app, set a mutual time limit (e.g., 30 mins for games).
- Explain the "why" rule. Teach them balance and that these devices are a privilege, not a right.
- 82% of parents see better behaviour with joint decisions.

## 03 Sit and Watch

- Honestly, the best thing you can do is watch and "try" to understand the game they are playing. You might be surprised with how skilled they are and might even spot the hidden benefits they could be learning from a certain game.
- Also, it makes things obvious if other players are interacting with your child. Sometimes it's best to be a silent observer and take mental notes of which games might be concerning you.

## 04 Weekly Review together

- Look at device reports together. This way we celebrate good days, tweak bad ones kindly, and reinforce positives by discouraging bad habits while focusing on wins.

## Nailed It: Your Camp's Secure!

Top effort! You've gone from jungle wanderer to camp master! These setups aren't set-and-forget. You can tweak as needed for that perfect balance. With 82% of parents stressing over safety, you're ahead of the pack. Feel the win: Safer kids, less worry, more family fun. You're smashing it!

> **"Controls aren't chains, they're safety nets for digital adventures."**

**Parents who model good habits cut kids' risk exposure by 50%. You're the secret weapon!**

# Modelling the Way: Be the Digital Role Model Your Kids Need

If setting up camp was about gearing up the tech, this one's the heart stuff:
Your habits are the blueprint for your kids to follow. Like teaching them to hold the door for someone, you lead, they copy.

No guilt trips here because we're all guilty of a late-night scroll. But realising 70% of Aussie kids mirror parents' screen behaviour means small changes pack a punch.

We'll hit self-checks, rules, zones, and pledges. So don't be caught "doom scrolling". Rise and shine as the role model by leading the way through your actions.

Why modelling? Kids learn more from what you do than what you say. eSafety notes that poor parent habits boost kids' risks, like endless scrolling leading to addiction vibes.
Positive examples build resilience, with 85% of families reporting better balance from shared rules. It's not about perfection; it's about progress.
Look to keep it simple; monkeys see, monkeys do! Now let's go!

## Let's Quiz You First!

Time for a bit of fun. Answer these 5 questions to spot your digital habits. Don't worry about where you land. This helps us realise how our behaviour rubs off.

| Questions | Yes | No | Sometimes |
|---|---|---|---|
| **Do you scroll during family meals or chats?** | | | |
| **Ever check work emails late at night with kids around?** | | | |
| **Do you share personal stuff online without thinking?** | | | |
| **Set screen limits for yourself, or wing it?** | | | |
| **Model kindness online (e.g., no troll comments)?** | | | |

**Scoring: Count Your "No"s and "Sometimes" Less Yeses the Better!**

| | |
|---|---|
| **5** | **Role Model Royalty, keep inspiring!** |
| **3-4** | **Solid Supporter, tweak for shine.** |
| **1-2:** | **Habit Tweaks needed, start small.** |
| **0:** | **Welcome; changes here pay off big.** |

If you're a "Doom Scroller," remember even superheroes have off days. Use results to pick one habit fix.

# Modelling Myths Busted

Let's bust some common myths about role modelling. These sneaky misconceptions can trip you up, but realising the truth makes it easier to lead by example without the pressure. No fluff, just facts to keep you on track.

- **Myth:** "I have to be a perfect digital saint, no slip-ups allowed."
  **Bust:** Nobody's perfect, and kids learn from how you handle mistakes too. A quick "Oops, I scrolled too long, let's both unplug now" shows resilience; research backs that honest recovery builds trust 50% faster than pretending you're flawless.
- **Myth:** "Teens are too independent; they won't notice or care what I do online."
  **Bust:** Wrong! They're watching closer than you think! Even rebellious teens mimic 70% of parent habits; your balanced screen time inspires theirs, cutting their risks without a word.
- **Myth:** "Rules and controls are enough; my own habits don't really matter."
  **Bust:** Tools help, but without your example, they're pointless. Positive modelling amps rules' effectiveness by 60%. When kids see you walk the talk, they follow suit naturally.
- **Myth:** "Is it too late to change if I've been a bad role model for years?"
  **Bust:** Never too late, my friend. Start small today, and kids adapt quickly. Families who tweak habits see improvements in weeks; it's progress over perfection, turning past slip-ups into teachable wins.

---

# Common Pitfalls & Quick Fixes

- **Pitfall:** "I try to be perfect but slip up" **Fix:** It's okay! Just acknowledge it, "Mum slipped up today, let's both try again tomorrow." Kids respect honesty.
- **Pitfall:** Kids say, "But you do it!" (I can even picture the tone in my head) **Fix:** Use it as a teaching moment, "You're right, I'm working on it too. Let's help each other."
- **Pitfall:** Teen resistance **Fix:** Give them some input, "What rule do you think would be fair?"

# Family Rules and Boundaries That Bond

Rules aren't restrictions; they're guardrails for safe fun. Start with 3-5 simple ones but make them stick. Families with rules see 60% less conflict. We all had rules growing up, so let's set some newer, with some up-to-date rules for kids these days.

Some examples of rules you could set up in your house for kids and parents to follow; it's really up to you the rules you put in place in your own household. So, I'll list a couple we found effective.

## Dinner Time

**No Devices at Dinner:**

Embrace Quality Time This guideline extends to turning off the TV, just as we used to do. Foster engaging conversations about school and other activities during mealtime.

## Bedtime Blackout

**Establishing Screen-Free Time Before Bed**

- Turn off screens 1 hour before bedtime.
- Consider taking it a step further by designating a specific area for all children's devices during this time. We use the kitchen bench where everything gets charged (easy to check also).

## Privilege not a Right

Through discussions with families while creating this book, I was surprised to discover how many children feel entitled to the technology we provide. Establishing this rule makes it clear that if they abuse that trust, it will be taken away!

## Tech-Free Zones

**Establish Areas where devices are "banned"**

- Designate areas for unplugging, such as the kitchen or bedrooms.
- Why is this important? It encourages spaces for conversation, establishes boundaries, and reminds everyone that devices don't need to be in their hands all the time.

## For Younger Kids (5-8)

- **Screens after homework only:** Helps focus.
- **Ask before sharing photos**: Builds privacy habits.
- **Bedtime story swap:** Device for book, helps winds down without fights.

## For Tweens (9-12)

- **No devices in bedrooms after 8pm**: cuts late-night temptations.
- **Check in on group chats daily**: spots bullying early.
- **Earn extra time with chores:** turns rules into rewards, like a points system.

## For Teens (13+)

- **Mute notifications during study time:** Boosts concentration.
- **Discuss posts before sharing:** Encourages thoughtful behaviour.
- **Weekly family unplugged night:** Reconnects offline, like a movie without phones.

## General All-Ages Winners

- **No secrets, tell if something's off online:** Builds trust.
- **Balance time: 1 hour play = 1 hour outside:** Fights addiction vibes.
- **Kindness code with positive comments only:** Models anti-bullying.

**Incorporate Children in Rulemaking**
**By involving kids in the process of creating rules, they are more likely to take ownership of them. Additionally, this approach fosters a sense of trust, making them feel valued and responsible.**

# Agreement Template:

Make it official with a family pledge: customise, sign, and stick it on the fridge. This builds accountability; 75% of families report better habits post-pledge. Think of it like when you were getting a pet and promised to pick up the poop, except your parents made you sign this to ensure you did. You can add a fun consequence, like "Breakers do the dishes!" (Extra Templates Page 107)

## Family Agreement

I, ..............................., the Kid/parent of ............................, have read and reviewed the Family Agreement for the Rules and Regulations for the device I'm about to receive. I acknowledge and agree to the following:

- [ ] I understand the responsibility of owning a phone.
- [ ] I recognise that I am not entitled to a phone and understand that this device can be taken away at any time.
- [ ] I will use screens for good by learning, laughing, and connecting only with people I know.
- [ ] I will only use my device at the times agreed upon with my parents.
- [ ] At any moment, my device may be subject to a random inspection, and I will willingly provide it without any hesitation.
- [ ] I agree to no secrets and I'll share if something's off online.

**Child Signature**
Name: ____________________

Signature: ____________________
Date: ____________________

**Adult Signature**
Name: ____________________

Signature: ____________________
Date: ____________________

# Outstanding work!

You're not just discussing safety; you're embodying it by establishing positive habits and a solid foundation.

**The Role of Rules**

Rules are crucial; they serve as guiding principles rather than restrictions on fun. Their significance is clear: shared rules reduce family conflicts, build trust, and install lasting self-control that carries into adulthood. Think of these rules as family values in action. When everyone commits, children come to understand that online safety is a collective effort, not just a parent's harsh rules.

**What If Kids Don't Follow?**

Don't worry if the kids resist; challenges are common but can be resolved without arguments. Begin with calm discussions: "What's causing the pushback? Often, it's frustration rather than rebellion."

- **Redirect Positively:** Instead of saying "No screens," suggest alternatives like "Let's play board games instead."
- **Natural Consequences:** If they break a rule, temporarily revoke a privilege, then reset the situation by praising their efforts.
- **Involve Them:** Collaborate on revising rules if they seem too strict.

**Remember**

Consistency is key: You're the captain navigating through the storms. Take pride in your efforts; your positive changes create ripples, leading to safer children and stronger family bonds. You've got this!

**"Be the change you want to see online, your kids are watching!"**

**Regular talks boost kids' confidence. 85% feel safer sharing issues with chat-ready parents!**

# Talking the Talk: Having Those Awkward Chats

With the habits and rules established already, it's time to tackle the tough conversations without the awkwardness. While no parent enjoys "the talk," a surprising 65% of Australians avoid it, leaving kids in the dark about potential risks. But don't worry!

I've hopefully got your back with:

- **Age-specific scripts:**
  Prepared lines for different age groups.
- **Role-play scenarios:**
  Practice what to do and what to avoid.
- **Warning Signs: Spot Trouble Early**
  Learn to recognise potential dangers.
- **Chat tracker journal:**
  Document and reflect on conversations.

These discussions build trust and can reduce grooming risks by 50%. Let's make these talks as easy as deciding what's for dinner.

# So Why Chat?

Silence can allow risks to go unnoticed, while open discussions empower children to identify dangers early, with 70% reporting issues sooner. I've tried to tailor these conversations to be age-appropriate by keeping them brief for younger kids and more in-depth for teenagers. It's okay to be nervous about these chats; we all remember them as kids ourselves.

# Age-Specific Scripts: Ready-to-Use Lines

Scripts help take the awkwardness out. Remember we are helping you take the lead if a situation arises, so keep calm and try to listen more than you talk.

**For 5–8 Year-Olds: Simple, story-like**

- On Strangers: "Same rules as if you are at a park; tell Mum or Dad first if a stranger reaches out, okay?"
- On Sharing: "Photos are special but ask me before sending them to anyone."
- On Upsets: "If something scary pops up, hit pause and come find me straight away; we'll fix it together."

**For 9-12 Year-Olds: Add why's.**

- On Bullying: "Mean messages hurt, block and tell me; it's not your fault."
- On Privacy: "Think before posting: Would you shout it in the playground?"
- On Grooming: "If someone asks for secrets or pics, that's a red flag, share with me pronto."

**For Teens (13+): Open questions.**

- On Sexting: "Pressure for nudes? Say no! It's illegal under 18; talk to me if unsure."
- On Misinformation: "Spot fakes: Check sources before sharing, let's discuss one."
- On Mental Health: "Social media blues? It's common, I'm here, no judgement."

**End with "What do you think?" turns monologue into dialogue.**

# Role-Play Scenarios (Do/Don't Examples)

Role-play builds confidence, like rehearsing a speech. Pick a scenario, act it out. Practise can cut awkwardness by 70%.

**DO'S**

**DON'TS**

| Scenario 1: Bullying Alert | |
|---|---|
| **Do's:** "If someone's mean online, like excluding you, tell me, we'll block and report together." (Empowers action.) | **Don'ts:** "The internet's full of monsters, stay off!" (Scares them silent.) |

| Scenario 2: Stranger Chat | |
|---|---|
| **Do's:** "If a new 'friend' asks personal stuff, that's dodgy. Show me the chat, no trouble." (Encourages insight.) | **Don'ts:** "Never talk to anyone online ever!" (Unrealistic.) |

| Scenario 3: Upsetting Content | |
|---|---|
| **Do's:** "Saw something yucky? It's not your fault; let's talk about how to avoid it next time." (Supports.) | **Don'ts:** "Why did you click that? Be careful!" (Blames.) |

> If it goes pear-shaped, don't stress; it's all a part of learning together!

## Timing Your Talks – When and How Often

Timing is everything; don't ambush your kid with a serious life lesson during a footy game! Start when they're relaxed, like after school or during a walk, and keep it regular to build trust without the drama. Consistent chats cut secrecy by 40%; aim for weekly check-ins, plus "as needed" for big events (e.g., new app download).

### Quick Tips for Timing:

- **Best Moments:** Car rides (captive audience, no eye contact pressure), bedtime wind-down (reflective mood), or family dinners (group vibe). Avoid: Right after school (hangry mode) or during favourite shows (distraction central).
- **How Often:** Little ones (5-8): Short daily nuggets, like "What was fun online today?" Tweens (9-12): Weekly deeper dives. Teens: Bi-weekly, plus open-door policy. Make it fun, not a chore.
- **How Long:** Keep under 10 minutes to start short and sweet; it builds habit without eye rolls.

### Chat Benefits Breakdown: The Payoff

Wondering if it's worth the awkward? Here's the upside:

- Builds Trust: Kids are 50% more likely to report issues.
- Boosts Resilience: Reduces bullying impact by 60%.
- Prevents Problems: Early talks cut exploitation risks by 80%.
- Strengthens Bonds: 85% of families report closer relationships.

> Like veggies, kids might not want them, but they grow strong kids!

## Overcoming Chat Barriers: When Kids Walled Up

Even with great scripts, kids might dodge conversations with "I don't want to talk!" and that's completely normal and fixable! With 65% of parents hitting this hurdle. But persistence pays off with trust and more openness between you and your child.

### Here's how to navigate the eye rolling:

**Barrier:** "It's embarrassing!"
**Fix:** Normalise with humour, "I felt awkward too at your age. Let's make it quick like ripping a band-aid." Start with low-stakes topics to build comfort.

**Barrier:** "You're always lecturing me!"
**Fix:** Listen first, then ask, "What's your take?" Use role-plays as games, not sermons; eSafety notes questions boost engagement by 70%.

**Barrier:** "Nothing's wrong!"
**Fix:** Watch for signs (page 43), gently probe with "Seen any funny memes lately?" to ease in. If shut down, try later. Timing is key in these moments.

**Barrier:** Cultural or Sensitivity Issues:
**Fix:** For diverse families, tie to personal values, "In our culture, we protect each other. Let's discuss how this extends to our online presence."

**TRUST** **RESILIENCE** **PREVENTION**

**Pro Tip:** If you notice multiple signs below, chat calmly and use scripts from earlier. Or reach out to hotlines if you're worried.

# Warning Signs: Spot Trouble Early

**Mood changes:** Snappy or withdrawn after screens? (Possible bullying.)

**What to Do:** Gently ask open questions like "Anything bothering you online?" This encourages sharing; if persistent, check device reports for clues and consider a family chat using scripts if needed.

**Secretive behaviour:** Hiding devices or clearing history? (Potential grooming or bullying.)

**What to Do:** Start a non-accusatory conversation. "Noticed you've been private with your phone; everything okay?" and review privacy settings together (Page 71).

**Sleep issues:** Up late online? (Possible addiction red flag.)

**What to Do:** Set bedtime blackouts via parental controls (Page 33) and model it yourself; if it's affecting school, track with the chat journal (Page 45) for patterns.

**Avoidance:** Dodging talks about online friends? (Possible hiding harms.)

**What to Do:** Use role-play scenarios (Page 40), to ease in indirectly; if avoidance continues, monitor for other flags and reach out to resources like Kids Helpline for advice.

**Physical signs:** Headaches from overuse? (Possible screen strain.)

**What to Do:** Encourage breaks by setting timers during screen time or tell them “Your eyes will turn square” like we were told; if linked to stress (e.g., bullying), combine with empathy support. (Page 50)

**Excessive time online:** Spending unusual hours on devices, especially at night?
(Increased exposure to risks like inappropriate content.)
**What to Do:** Use device reports to spot patterns and set daily limits (page 21,33); discuss as a family to redirect energy to offline hobbies, building resilience.

**Receiving unknown gifts or messages:** Getting calls, packages, or items from strangers?
(Potential grooming or exploitation.)
**What to Do:** Ask calmly about the source and report suspicious contacts to eSafety immediately; block the sender and review app privacy to prevent future outreach.

**Falling grades or lost interests:** Dropping school performance or ditching hobbies?
(Possible cyberbullying or addiction impact.)
**What to Do:** Connect it to online habits with a gentle check-in "Noticed school's been tough; anything online adding stress?" and use the 30-day challenge (Page 87) to rebuild balance.

**Be aware that potential issues and possible causes may differ from what your child is currently experiencing. These warning signs are intended to keep you vigilant about potential dangers.**

# Chat Tracker Journal

## Log and Learn

We'll dive deeper into this when we get to the 30-day challenge section (page 87). But I wanted to note here that Monitoring and Tracking discussions can really help reveal patterns and insights that can simplify future interactions. Additionally, it helps identify recurring events that may require escalation.

For example, if your child notes a particular bully online multiple times, then escalation is the obvious next step.

You could even turn it into a weekly thing. Reviewing the week's entries and then focusing your next steps on studying the topic discussed and the ways to address these issues.

For an example of how you might write something down:

- Date/Topic: "10/2/26, Bullying discussion."
- Child's Response: "Felt okay, asked questions."
- Wins/Next Steps: "Good listener; follow up on app blocks."
- Patterns Noted: "Third time mentioning mean comments, check school involvement?"
- Escalation Check: "No red flags yet, but monitor mood next week."
- My Confidence Level: "4/5, handled well, but could listen more."

You can customise this however you need, even add emojis if needed. The goal of this is for it to become your secret weapon when it comes to protecting your child. But remember to document the good as well and try to celebrate wins with the kids.

No pressure, you can start small, but once you see the insights and progress begin to reveal themselves, you will see why I added this.

**Fact:** Journaling boosts chat consistency by 40%, turning random check-ins into a reliable habit.

# Chat Master Class: You've Got the Words

Brilliant! You're now equipped to turn awkward into awesome! These tools make talks a habit, reducing risks and strengthening bonds. Feel the power: Open and honest conversations help kids navigate safely.

> **Awkward today, confident tomorrow; your words shape their world.**

53% of kids face online bullying, but support helps 80% bounce back stronger!

# Spotting the Snakes: Recognizing and Handling Cyberbullying

Addressing Cyberbullying: The Hidden Threat
With things now flowing from those awkward chats, it's time to confront the sneakiest threat: cyberbullying, affecting 53% of Australian children like a preventable bluebottle sting.

No Need to Worry!
We'll equip you with:

- Types of cyberbullying
- Support tips
- Where to report issues you face

With research indicating that with early action, you can reduce long-term harm by 70%. You're the family's snake charmer in this situation. Let's navigate this challenge together!

Why focus on bullying? It's not just "kids being kids" online. It hits harder, with 24/7 access amplifying the situation and the hurt. eSafety reports 1 in 2 young Aussies are affected, but recognising signs lets you step in early. No blame; we're all learning.

## Types of Cyberbullying

Understanding different types of bullying helps you respond in the right way, with 53% of incidents occurring on social media alone. Here's a detailed overview, ranging from mild to severe:

- **Trolling/Teasing:** Mean-spirited jokes, such as mocking posts. *(Yellow alert: Often starts innocently but can escalate.)*
- **Exclusion**: Leaving individuals out of groups or chats. *(Orange: Damages feelings of belonging; accounts for 30% of cases.)*
- **Doxxing/Harassment**: Distributing private information or relentless attacks. *(Red: Highly dangerous; report immediately.)*
- **Impersonation**: Fake accounts pretending to be someone else. *(Red: Resembles identity theft; affects 15% of individuals.)*

## MYTHS VS FACTS

| | |
|---|---|
| "Its just kids being kids, harmless fun." | **No way;** 53% affected suffer real hurt (anxiety, low self-esteem). It's serious! Report to stop it spreading. |
| "It only happens on social media." | **Wrong;** games/apps like Roblox see 30% of cases. Check all platforms; filters cut exposure by 70%. |
| "Victims bring it on themselves." | **Blame game is a no-go;** bullies choose their targets. Instead, fostering Support builds resilience, 80% recover with empathy. |
| "Ignoring it makes it go away." | **Often worsens;** 40% escalate without action. Block/report empowers; involve schools for backup. |

## Support and Empathy: Heal the Hurt

If bullying hits, support first and then listen without rushing to fix the situation. The fact is that empathy reduces emotional scars by 60%. These exercises build resilience.

- Listen Actively: "Tell me more, I'm here." Why? Validates feelings; 80% of kids open up more.
- Rebuild Confidence: Praise strengths offline. For example, "You're ace at footy; let's focus there."
- Role-Reverse: "How would you help a mate?" Teaches perspective.

## Building Bully-Proof Resilience: Prevention Tips for Parents

Spotting snakes is great, but preventing bites is better! eSafety says building resilience cuts cyberbullying impact by 70%. These tips focus on emotional armour at home, empowering your kid without the fuss.

- **Encourage Open Sharing:** Make "online check-ins" routine, like "What's the best/worst thing you saw today?"
  **Why?** Boosts trust; kids are 50% more likely to report early harms.

- **Teach Kindness Online:** Role-model positive posts (e.g., "Compliment a mate's pic") and discuss "digital footprints."
  **Why?** Reduces bullying participation; there are 60% fewer incidents in kind-focused families.

- **Promote Offline Balance:** Set "unplugged adventures" (e.g., park days), limit screens to 2 hours of fun time.
  **Why?** Strong offline bonds buffer online hurts; resilient kids recover 80% faster.

- **Build Self-Esteem:** Praise non-screen wins (e.g., "Ace job on that drawing!") to counter mean comments.
  **Why?** High self-esteem drops bullying effects by 50%; they're less likely to be targeted.

## How To Team Up Against Bullying

You don't fight snakes alone. I've already got your back with this book, but you can also loop in schools or members of the community for extra muscle. eSafety says partnered responses resolve 75% of cases faster. It's like calling the snake catcher; leave it to the pros to handle the venom!

- **Talk to Teachers:** Share evidence; most schools have anti-bullying policies. **Why?** Coordinated help stops the spread; 60% resolved quicker.
- **Use Community Resources:** Join local parent groups or eSafety webinars. **Why?** Shared stories build support; it reduces isolation for kids.
- **School Reporting Steps:** Notify via email/form; follow up. **Why?** Legal backing if needed; it empowers your response.

- **Long-Term Teamwork:** Suggest school programmes like peer mentoring. **Why?** Prevents recurrence; resilient communities cut bullying by 50%.

## Reporting Evidence and eSafety Steps

Don't let bullies win. Report to stop it spreading. Reporting resolves 70% of cases. Tick if needed.

☐ **Gather Evidence:** Screenshots, dates, URLs, save safely.
☐ **Talk to School:** If school-related, notify teachers.
☐ **Block/Report on App:** Use built-in tools (e.g., Instagram report button).
☐ **eSafety Hotline:** Call 1800 880 176 or use the online form for serious issues.
☐ **Local Police if Threats:** For doxxing/harassment, call triple zero if urgent.

## Snake-Spotter! You are smashing it!

Top-notch! You're now equipped to spot and squash cyberbullying like a pro! By recognising types, offering support, and reporting smartly, you're shielding your family from hidden harms. Remember, 53% face It, but your actions make the difference; early intervention boosts recovery and prevents repeat incidents.

You should feel empowered; this knowledge turns scary into solvable. Stay vigilant and proactive, and remember that you're not alone in this fight. Encourage open conversations within your family about online experiences, and ensure everyone knows they can reach out for help at any time. Empower your kids to stand up for others online; by reporting and sharing concerns with you, so we can create a safer online environment for everyone. Keep learning, stay connected, and together we can stand strong against cyberbullying and create a safer digital world for all.

> **"Spot the snakes, strike with support and be the family's guardian!**

WARNING

# When the Snake is in Your Own Nest: If Your Child is Bullying Others

This is one of the hardest sections any parent will read. And a subject not many people like to cover. Discovering that your own child is the one doing the bullying can feel like a punch to the gut. The shock, the guilt, the "how did I miss this?" questions that keep you up at night are all normal. No one wants to believe their kid could be the bully. But here you are.

And the fact that you're still reading shows how much you love them and how much you want to do the right thing. This section of the book is written with zero judgement, only support.

Good kids sometimes do bad things online. The important part is what happens next. Let's walk through this together, calmly and honestly.

# Why this conversation needs to happen:

Finding out your child is bullying others is incredibly painful. Many parents describe feelings shown below.

**All of these feelings are valid.**

You are not a bad parent for feeling them.

The truth is, bullying online often happens because of things like peer pressure, stress at school, wanting to fit in, or not fully understanding how much their words or jokes can hurt when there's a screen between them.

It doesn't mean your child is a bad person; it just means they need guidance right now. So, we are aiming to give you that guidance first, so you can pass it onto them.

# Red Flags That Your Child Might Be Bullying Others

These signs are different from the ones you look for when your child is being bullied. Watch for patterns, not single incidents.

- Sudden defensiveness when you ask about their online friends or group chats
- Spending a lot of time laughing at or sharing "roasts," memes, or drama about other kids
- Receiving praise or gifts from peers for being "funny" or "savage" online
- Quickly deleting messages or switching apps when you walk into the room
- Using more sarcastic, cruel, or dismissive language at home
- Showing little empathy when you mention someone being bullied at school
- Bragging about "winning" arguments online or getting someone blocked/banned
- Having multiple accounts or "insta" profiles that they keep hidden from you

**What to Do if You Spot These Flags:** Stay calm. Don't accuse straight away. Take a breath, gather some evidence if needed, and prepare for an honest conversation with the scripts coming up.

# What to Do in the First 24–48 Hours

The first hours after discovery are the hardest. Your priority is staying calm so you can support your child and take the right steps.

1

**Stay Calm First**
Take a moment for yourself. Walk around the block, have a cuppa, call a trusted friend. Your child needs you steady, not spiralling.

2

**Gather Evidence Privately**
Screenshots of messages/posts. Save them somewhere your child can't delete.

3

**Have the First Difficult Conversation**
Choose a quiet time. Start with: "I saw some messages that really worried me. I love you, and I want to understand what's going on."

4

**Listen Before You Speak**
Let them talk. Many kids feel ashamed once they realise the impact. Your calm listening is powerful.

5

**Take Immediate Safety Steps**

- Serious Review of apps and Family Agreement
- Contact the school if it's happening there
- For serious incidents, contact your Local Police

# Starting the Conversation with Ready to use Scripts

Here are three calm ways to begin. Adapt them to your child's age and personality, and feel free to tweak them however you need. The goal is to open the door, not slam it shut.

## Soft opener

**(Perfect for younger kids or high emotions)**

"Hey, I saw something on your phone that worried me. I'm not angry at all, I just want to understand what's going on. Can we talk about it?"

## Fact-based opener

**(Works well for tweens and teens)**

"I saw some posts and messages that don't seem like you. It looks like someone might have been hurt by them. I'm not angry, but I really need to understand what happened."

## Curious opener

**(Great for reducing defensiveness)**

"I noticed some messages that concerned me. I'd really like to hear your side of what was happening. I'm here to listen, no judgement at all."

This first conversation sets the tone for everything that follows. Stay steady, stay kind, and remember, you're not a bad parent for having this talk. You're a good parent for doing it.

## Extra Delivery Tips:

- Keep your voice calm and low, no shouting or accusing tone.
- Start with love or care: "I'm worried because I care about you."
- Listen more than you talk at first. Let them explain. Many kids feel ashamed once they realise the impact; your calm listening is powerful.
- If they shut down, say: "It's okay if you're not ready to talk right now. I'm here when you are."

See if you notice these approaches in the conversations below.

---

## Fake Scenarios You Could Face and How to Handle It

These scenarios are crafted as practical "what if" role-plays. As you read through them, take a moment to reflect on your feelings in that moment and consider how you would respond to the situation being presented.

**Ask yourself questions like:**

- Is the parent doing enough?
- Is their tone and approach effective?
- Would I have done it differently?

### Fake Scenario One:
### 13-year-old son in a cruel group chat

You open your son's phone and discover he's been sending nasty messages and memes about a classmate. Your heart drops and guilt hits hard. You take a deep breath and sit with him calmly: "I saw the messages. They're really hurtful. Help me understand what was going on." You listen first, then explain the impact. As a natural consequence of your family rules (page 33), you remove the group chat app for two weeks and tighten screen-time limits using the tools from the (page 21). You also contact the school counsellor together the next day. Within a month, he's apologised and the group has stopped.

## Scenario 2:
## 14-year-old son
## excluding and mocking a boy

You find out through the school that your son has been part of a group excluding and mocking another boy offline at the school and through online messages to friends. You feel angry at yourself for not noticing sooner. You sit with him that evening and say, "I've heard some things that worry me. Let's talk about what's been happening." You use a calm conversation approach from the (page 57). As a consequence, you remove gaming privileges for a week (Page 33) and contact eSafety together to remove harmful posts (Page 51). You discuss options with the school. He writes a genuine apology and gives it to the boy at school. Six months later, he's much kinder online.

---

## Scenario 3:
## 16-year-old daughter
## sending vicious messages

Your 16-year-old daughter has been part of a group sending vicious messages that led to another girl self-harming. At her age, she's very independent with her phone, so you feel helpless at first. You take a moment to compose yourself, then sit with her and say, "I saw the messages and this is serious. I love you, but we need to sort this out together." You use the calm conversation approach from the relevant (Page 57). You contact the school the next morning, reach out to eSafety for content removal, and book family counselling through Headspace. As a natural consequence, you set clear open-phone agreements (Page 35), and she loses certain social media apps for a month. She's since taken full responsibility and your relationship is stronger than ever.

# Guiding Your Child Back Accountability Without Shame

Your goal is to guide your child with accountability and growth, not to punish them until they feel broken.

- **Start with a calm, private conversation,** Sit side-by-side (not face-to-face) so it feels less like an interrogation and use a gentle opener like: "I saw what happened and it worries me because I know you're better than this. Help me understand what was going on for you."
- **Listen first, really listen,** Let them speak without jumping in to correct or lecture. Your calm listening shows them it's safe to be honest with you.
- Then **help them understand** the real impact with simple reflective questions such as: "How do you think that made the other person feel?" or "What would you feel if someone did that to you?" This builds empathy without shaming.
- **Apply natural consequences** that teach rather than just punish, for example, a temporary loss of the app where it happened. Clearly explain why: "This isn't forever. It's so you can think about what happened and choose better next time."
- **Guide a genuine apology together**, not a forced "sorry," but a real one like "I realise what I said hurt you and I'm really sorry. I won't do that again."
- If the behaviour continues or feels too big to handle alone, seeking help from a school counsellor or psychologist is a wise and loving choice.

You're teaching your child how to be a better person and showing them, they are still loved and supported, even after making mistakes.

# Prevention So It Doesn't Happen Again

With the immediate crisis under control, focus on creating lasting change in your family's online culture.

- **Revise Family Rules:** Emphasise kindness and respect in simple, visible rules agreed upon together.
- **Build Daily Habits:** Conduct regular check-ins asking about online experiences to keep communication open.
- **Model Behaviour:** Demonstrate desired online conduct, showing kindness and putting devices away during family time.
- **Encourage Offline Activities:** Schedule screen-free activities to strengthen real-world connections.
- **Celebrate Positive Choices:** Praise your child for kind actions online to reinforce good behaviour.
- **Learn Together:** Engage in discussions about digital respect through videos and articles to normalise these conversations.

Creating a family culture of online kindness takes consistency and patience, leading to more thoughtful and responsible children.

---

> **"Even when they make mistakes, our children still deserve our love and guidance, not because they earned it, but because they need it.**

# You're Not Alone! Support for You, the Parent

Discovering your child has been involved in something can bring a wave of shock, guilt, fear, and even shame. But online bullying is taken very seriously; in some cases, it can lead to police involvement or criminal charges for the young person involved. That's why acting calmly and quickly matters so much. Please hear this clearly: This doesn't make you a bad parent. It makes you a parent who loves their child enough to face this painful truth and do the right thing. You don't have to carry this alone. There are kind, experienced people and services ready to support both you and your child right now. Reaching out for help is a sign of strength, not failure.

Below are trusted Australian services that understand exactly what you're going through:

- **Parentline (1300 30 1300)** Free, confidential phone support for parents in every state. They specialise in helping mums and dads navigate tough situations like this, no judgement, just practical advice and emotional support.
- **Kids Helpline (1800 55 1800)** 24/7 support for children and young people, but parents can also call for guidance on how to talk to their child and manage their own feelings.
- **eSafety Commissioner (1800 880 176 or esafety.gov.au)** Specialist advice on online bullying and harmful content. They can help with content removal and give clear next steps for parents in your situation.
- **Beyond Blue (1300 22 4636 or beyondblue.org.au)** Mental health support for parents feeling overwhelmed, anxious, or down. You can speak to someone about the guilt and stress you're carrying.
- **Headspace (headspace.org.au)** Youth mental health services that also support families. Many centres offer family counselling when a young person has been involved in bullying.
- **Your Child's School Counsellor** Often the first and most practical place to start. They know your child and can coordinate support between home and school.

## Message of Hope

You've faced one of parenting's toughest challenges: discovering your child is causing harm online. This reality brings guilt and fear, but your willingness to confront it shows your love and commitment. The book aims to guide you on protecting your child and hopefully helps you navigate this difficult situation.

Many families emerge stronger from these challenges through honest conversations. You have the tools and heart to guide your child. Take it day by day and be the loving parent you aspire to be.

> **Remember, I've said it over and over, but you are not a bad parent; you're brave for seeking growth and support.**

60% of Aussies fall for scams yearly, but privacy smarts slash that risk in half!

# Privacy Pirates: Protecting Personal Info and Avoiding Scams

Ahoy, treasure guardians! It's time to protect ourselves from the cunning pirates who seek to steal personal information. With 25% of children experiencing harassment from oversharing, there's no need to worry; we'll tackle passwords, scams, pledges, and app guides together. Think of this part of the book as us cleanning up your treasure map to make sure only your family can access the treasure. Statistics reveal that robust privacy measures can reduce scams by 90%; you are the captain navigating these safe waters. Let's raise the sails!

**Why Pirate-Proof?**

Oversharing can lead to issues, eSafety reports that 1 in 4 children face online harassment due to leaked information. However, adopting simple practices like using strong passwords can change the game. There's no need for paranoia; just smart navigation.

> Your password isn't something like "123456," is it? If so, you might need more help than this guide can provide.

# Password and Authenticator Basics: Lock Your Loot

Let's start with the basics. Weak passwords are the easiest habit to change, and with 2FA and suggested passwords, there is no excuse for leaving any account vulnerable with a lazy password. So let's go over some things you could do to make things better already.

## Password Strength Levels:

| Weak | Okay | Strong |
|---|---|---|
| "password123" hacked in seconds. Avoid! | "MyDogSpot2026" better, but predictable. | "P1r@teSh1p$Au55ie!" mix caps, numbers, symbols, unique per site. |

## Extra Tips

**Passwords**
Use managers like Samsung Pass or Passkey

**Two-Factor Authentication**
Enable 2FA everywhere, using a text code or app.

**Hacked?**
Change after breaches emails or suspicious activity

# Protecting You and Your Kids:

While I can discuss various ways to protect your children, it's essential to connect this back to you being the role model for them by setting a positive example. Now is an excellent opportunity to review your own privacy settings, ensuring your profile is set to private or friends-only. You might be surprised by how many parents share details about birthdays and pets, where you were born... Do you see where I'm going with this? It's not hard to guess your security questions if you post the answers online.

# Passcodes and Locks

Every device in the house, **yours included**, should have a strong passcode or biometric lock. This is one of the simplest and most effective privacy defences you can have.

Decide early what kind of rule fits your family:

- **Trust approach:** (great for older kids and teens) They know the passcode, but you have an open agreement that you can ask to see the device anytime, and they'll hand it over without drama.
- **Strict approach:** (better for younger kids or higher-risk situations) Only you know the passcode. You unlock it when needed and always explain why.

## Next-level option:
## Add your fingerprint or Face ID

Many parents choose a middle path by adding their own fingerprint (or Face ID) to their child's device alongside the child's passcode. This means you can unlock the phone instantly if needed, while your child still has their own access for daily use.

It's a great compromise for families who want quick access without fully taking over the device. Just be upfront with your child: "I've added my fingerprint so I can help if something goes wrong; it's about safety, not spying."

Whichever approach you choose, be consistent and explain the "why" to your child. A clear passcode rule gives you quick access when you need it, while still teaching healthy boundaries and trust around technology.

**Don't forget to change your own lock code every few months; I feel like I'm not the only one who sees kids pick up parents' phones and know the password off by heart. Boundaries apply to your own technology too.**

# Scam Spotter Game:

Fun quiz to train your eye, let's play Scam or Legit on common scams. Spotting early saves 80% from losses. Play with family!

|  | | |
|---|---|---|
| Free V-Bucks offer in Fortnite chat? | Scam? | Legitimate? |
| **Scam!** False freebies, official sites only. | | |
| Bank email asking for password? | Scam? | Legitimate? |
| **Scam!** Banks never ask; call them directly. | | |
| Friend's DM for gift card help? | Scam? | Legitimate? |
| **Maybe scam,** verify offline; 40% impersonation | | |
| Pop-up 'Virus alert' saying pay to fix? | Scam? | Legitimate? |
| **Scam!** Fake alerts, run free scans instead. | | |
| Unknown link in text? | Scam? | Legitimate? |
| **No!** Phishing links steal info; delete. | | |

# Its time to Double Down

It's crucial to discuss common scams with your family, such as those mentioned above. However, given the constantly evolving nature of the internet, scammers will continually adapt and devise new and creative tactics to deceive you. Therefore, use this guide to remain vigilant online and to create habits that you can follow and watch out for.

# Why Scammers Target Kids

Scammers don't go after kids because they're cruel. They do it because it's easy money.

Children are goldmines for them. Kids freely share names, ages, schools, photos, locations, and often have parents' credit cards saved in games. Scammers know that many families have payment methods linked to devices and kids usually don't understand the risks.

**What they're really after:**

- Your child's personal information to build fake profiles
- Access to saved payment methods for silent purchases
- Photos and videos they can use for blackmail (sextortion)
- Control of the device to spread malware or steal from the whole family

If a child's device gets hacked, scammers can quietly drain linked bank accounts, steal family photos, impersonate your child to trick friends, or even use the camera and microphone without anyone knowing. In some cases, they lock the device and demand ransom. It can happen faster than most parents realise, sometimes in minutes. But here's the good news: almost all of this can be stopped with the simple protections we've covered in this Section.

# The Scary Truth: Predators and Grooming

Scammers aren't the only danger online. Predators also target children because it's easy to build trust quickly. Kids often accept friend requests from strangers in games like Roblox, Fortnite, or Discord. What starts as friendly chatting can slowly turn into grooming, gaining your child's trust, asking for photos, and eventually trying to move the conversation offline or arrange to meet in person. This is exactly why strong privacy settings, private profiles, and the clear family rule "never accept friend requests from strangers" are so important.

The tools and habits in this parts are designed to close those doors before anyone can even start knocking.

# App Settings Guide: Seal the Hatches

Many apps already contain great privacy settings built into them; it's just a matter of turning them on and getting them fine-tuned to seal up any leaks you could run into. I'll go over some below that we set up on the kids' devices that work great.

| App | Protection Setup |
|---|---|
| **TikTok** | Set to Private Account (Profile > Settings > Privacy > Private Account); enable Family Pairing (Settings > Family Pairing) for parent oversight on comments/duets. |
| **Instagram** | Set to Private (Profile > Settings > Privacy > Private Account); restrict DMs (Settings > Privacy > Messages > Allow Messages From > Friends). |
| **Snapchat** | Turn on Ghost Mode (Settings > See My Location > Off); enable Friend Requests only from contacts (Settings > Who Can > Contact Me > My Friends). |
| **Roblox** | Activate Account Restrictions (Settings > Security > Enable); set Chat to Friends Only (Settings > Privacy > Who can chat with me > Friends). |
| **YouTube** | Enable Restricted Mode (Settings > General > Restricted Mode > On); turn off personalised ads (Google Account > Data & Privacy > Ad Settings > Off). |
| **Facebook** | Set profile to Friends Only (Settings > Privacy > Who can see your posts > Friends); enable Login Alerts (Settings > Security > Get alerts about unrecognised logins > On). |

Whether it's hiding videos and guarding posts from strangers, or hiding and filtering things you and the kids might not want to see, if you knuckle down on this part of anything from the book, it will be most beneficial, I hope.

## Social media privacy

- **Be Mindful of Sharing:** Pause before posting. Skip addresses, routines, or kid details; opt out of biometrics (e.g., face scans in Reels). Why? It minimises "digital footprints." Not to freak you out, but if your profile is public and you upload photos of your kids, anyone can save those photos and use them.
- **Manage Ads and Tracking:** Disable personalised ads (Google: Ad Settings › Off; Apple: Settings › Privacy › Tracking › Off). Why? It slashes data harvesting by 50%; AI ads target kids sneakily, but this setting should solve most of your "I think my phone is listening to me" conversations.
- **Practice Safe Browsing:** Use VPNs on public Wi-Fi, verify "https" sites, and avoid dodgy links. Why? It dodges phishing; always check URLs.

## Kid Specific Setups

Aussie kids have the new under-16 bans and age verification on TikTok, Snapchat, and more apps to come. But be careful of children not creating accounts at all and surfing sites and games, making it even more dangerous if they do it now.

- **Family Accounts & Controls:** Set to private, use tools like Instagram's Family Centre for monitoring. Why? It blocks unknowns; teach kids to report or block suspicious users to empower them.
- **Limit Data Sharing:** Disable geo-tags and avoid including school or kid details in posts. Why? This prevents regrets; discuss "digital footprints" with teens, eSafety says this cuts future harms.
- **Stay Updated:** The eSafety Website constantly updates you with new scams and skills for you to keep ahead of the game.

## Ads & Loot Boxes: Traps in Kid's Game's

In "free" kids' games, ads run wild, as you've probably seen. They offer a mix of flashy promotions for other games or in-game goodies that turn fun into financial or privacy pitfalls. You only need to look at any game to see the bombardment kids experience.

Now, some kids will sit through the one-minute ad for another life, but let's say a deliberate or accidental purchase is made and your card's linked to a child's device without safeguards; one tap racks up surprise bills. But it's okay, I'll list some measures to keep things safe without altogether needing to ban the fun.

## Dangers Lurking in Ads & Loot Boxes:

- **Impulse Purchases & Financial Sneak Attacks:** Kids click "buy now" for virtual items (skins, coins), saved cards lead to $100+ shock bills; eSafety reports that spends rack up fast.
- **Data Harvesting:** Ads track habits to push targeted tricks, sharing info with marketers; this boosts scam exposure (60% of Aussies are hit yearly).
- **Phishing Bait:** Fake "free upgrade" ads hide malware/links that steal details; 21% experience it, according to the ABS.
- **Gambling Gateway & Addiction Hooks:** Loot boxes mimic pokies, users pay for mystery rewards, normalising betting; users are 6 times more prone to problems, according to eSafety.

## Seal the Traps: Quick Safeguards

- **Use Virtual/Prepaid Cards:** Link low-limit ones (Apple Pay/Google Wallet, $20 cap), protects the main account from impulse hits.
- **Disable In-App Purchases:** iOS (Screen Time › Content Restrictions › iTunes Purchases › Off); Android (Play Store › Require Auth), blocks purchases outright.
- **Ad Blockers & Restricted Mode:** Enable in apps like YouTube Gaming; use family-safe browsers to filter junk.
- **Game Reviews First:** Always make it a habit to check the review section first. As you would for a real purchase, if there are low reviews, then skip it!

# Pirate-Proofed: Your Info's Safe!

Treasure secured! You've navigated privacy like a pro captain! These tools fend off pirates, giving peace in choppy digital seas.
Feel the strength: Protected info means more freedom online.

## Quick Parent Checklist:

- ☐ MFA on?
- ☐ Profiles private?
- ☐ Ads off?
- ☐ Kids know report/block?
- ☐ Geo-tags disabled?
- ☐ Card virtual only?
- ☐ IAPs off?
- ☐ Games eSafety-checked?
- ☐ Kids know the risks?

**"Guard your gold, privacy's the real treasure!"**

74% of kids encounter inappropriate content, but talks and tools help 80% navigate safely!

# The Dark Side: Dealing with Exploitation and Inappropriate Content

Building on the knowledge you've gained so far, we shine a light on the shadows: There's no need for fearmongering; I've got you covered with insights on red flags, reporting, recovery, and resources to help. Research shows that taking proactive measures can protect 80% of children; you can be their guiding light.

So let's teach you how to shine.

You might still be asking why you need to confront the darkness. It's simple: Ignoring these issues only increases risks. eSafety indicates that exposure to pornography or grooming can hinder development, but early intervention can lead to healing. Approach this with care: Emphasise support over shame. Think of it like checking under the bed for monsters, most of the time, there's nothing there, but it's better to be safe!

What We'll Explore:

- Red flags and scenarios: Identifying them early.
- Reporting and recovery steps: Creating actionable plans.
- Professional help resources: Where to seek assistance.
- Conclusion: Building resilience.

# Red Flags and Scenarios: Shining a Light Early

Flags serve as your early warning system with 14% of kids experience grooming, and 74% encounter inappropriate content. Recognizing these signs allows for swift action.

| Red Flag | Description | Possible Cause |
|---|---|---|
| Sudden secrecy with devices | Hiding screens, deleting history, or using incognito mode more often. | Grooming or hiding exposure to harms. |
| Unexplained gifts or items | Receiving packages, money, or online credits from "friends." | Abusers use favours to build trust. |
| Frequent contact from unknown people | Getting messages/calls in multiple ways (e.g., app, text, email). | Groomers push for constant connection to isolate. |
| Mood shifts | Anxious, angry, or depressed after online time. | Impact from abuse or content. |
| Spending more time away or missing routines | Skipping school, activities, or being secretive about whereabouts. | Meeting online contacts offline. |
| Misusing substances | Sudden alcohol/drug use linked to online stress. | Coping with trauma from exploitation. |
| Relationship with much older "friend" | Chatting with adults who act overly friendly or romantic. | Grooming tactic to gain influence. |
| Sexual health concerns | Developing issues like infections or questions about adult topics. | From coerced acts or exposure. |

# Real Scenarios and ways to approach it.

| Scenario | Description / Response |
| --- | --- |
| **Grooming Online** | A "friendly" stranger in a game builds trust with compliments, then asks for personal pics or secrets. |
| | Response: Block immediately, save evidence, report to eSafety hotline; this cuts escalation by 90%. |
| **Accidental Porn Exposure** | A "friendly" stranger in a game builds trust with compliments, then asks for personal pics or secrets. |
| | Response: Reassure it's not their fault, enable stricter filters (Page 71) and discuss safe browsing. |
| **Image Abuse (Sextortion)** | Shared pic gets manipulated or threatened to be spread unless they send more. |
| | Response: Don't pay/send more; report to eSafety for removal (handles 90% fast), seek Kids Helpline support. |
| **Online to Offline Meetup** | Child plans to meet an "online mate" who's much older, often after gifts or promises. |
| | Response: Intervene gently, explain risks, block contact, involve police if a meet-up occurred. eSafety says secrecy is a key flag. |
| **Deepfake Deception** | Fake video/image of the child (using AI) circulates, causing distress. |
| | Response: Report to eSafety for takedown; discuss digital footprints (without blame) to prevent future shares. |

Take a moment to consider how you would feel discovering something concerning on your child's device; it can be quite overwhelming, so it's important to stay calm. Although it may seem unusual to focus on this during such a moment, it's crucial for your child to understand that they can approach you when these situations arise and feel secure in doing so.

## Reporting and Recovery Steps

Report to stop spread, eSafety handles 90% of cases fast.

**Reporting Steps:**

- Gather evidence: Screenshots, URLs safely.
- Block then contact eSafety: Hotline 1800 880 176 or online.
- Involve school/police if needed: For threats.
- Follow up: Check status with officials.

## What to do after an incident

**Reassure:**

"It's not your fault; we'll fix this." (Builds trust.)

**Limit Exposure:**

Tighten controls, therapy if impacted. (70% recover fully with support.)

**Rebuild Positives:**

Focus on safe online fun. (Restores confidence.)

**“Pro Tip: Monitor gently in these moments; overdoing can backfire.**

This book aims to raise your awareness of specific situations and to remind you that if they arise, you shouldn't face them alone. These services are free and confidential.

**Fact:** Seeking help early can resolve 70% of issues.

# Empathy Toolkit: Supporting Your Kid Through the Shadows

When the dark side hits, empathy's your secret torch. With supportive responses, you can speed recovery by 70%, helping kids feel secure without shame. These quick tools focus on emotional mending, turning tough moments into growth.

**These can be adapted any way you like:**

- **Validation Exercise:** Say "I believe you, and it's not your fault," and repeat in a quiet spot. Why? It validates feelings; kids are 60% more likely to open up next time.
- **Safe Space Ritual:** Create a "no-judgement zone" (e.g., couch corner) for talks. Why? It builds trust and reduces anxiety from incidents like grooming exposure.
- **Strength Spotlight:** List 3 non-online strengths (e.g., "You're ace at drawing") together. Why? It rebuilds self-esteem and counters harm's emotional toll.
- **Breathing Buddy:** Guide slow breaths (in for 4, hold for 4, out for 4) during upset. Why? It calms immediate stress; eSafety notes it helps 50% manage trauma better.

# Resilience Rebuild Plan: Bouncing Back Stronger

After the shadows, rebuild like a boss. eSafety talks about how structured plans help speed healing by 50%, turning incidents into lessons. These steps focus on family routines to help bounce back, no therapy deep-dive needed. Think of it like a boomerang: throw it out, and it comes back tougher!

- **Step 1:** Daily Positives: Note one good thing daily (e.g., "Fun offline game"). Why? Shifts focus; rebuilds joy post-harm.
- **Step 2:** Routine Reset: Add one safe habit (e.g., "Evening unplugged hour"). Why? Restores balance; cuts re-exposure by 60%.
- **Step 3:** Strength Sessions: Weekly family "win shares" on non-online skills. Why? Boosts esteem; resilient kids handle 80% better.
- **Step 4:** Progress Track: Log improvements in a simple chart. Why? Sees growth; motivates ongoing vigilance.

# Dark Side Myths Busted: Facing Facts Without Fear

Myths can dim your torch, we have to bust them to stay lit! eSafety says debunking helps parents act 60% faster on harms like grooming. These focus on exploitation truths, no panic, just clear sailing.

- **Myth:** "It only happens to 'bad' kids online."
  **Fact:** Wrong! Any child can be targeted; 14% groomed randomly. Proactive filters/teaching cut chances by 80%.
- **Myth:** "One exposure won't hurt."
  **Fact:** No! Repeated views impact development; 74% see harms accidentally. Fact: Quick recovery builds resilience for life.
- **Myth:** "Parents can't really help after it happens."
  **Fact:** False! You're key; supportive steps heal in 70% of cases. Fact: Report/remove content fast via eSafety.
- **Myth:** "It's rare in Australia."
  **Fact:** Nah! Local stats match global; under-16 bans help, but vigilance is vital. Community action prevents escalations.

---

# Professional Help Resources: Lifelines Ready

- **eSafety Commissioner:** esafety.gov.au / 1800 880 176 (Reports/removals).
- **Kids Helpline:** kidshelpline.com.au / 1800 55 1800 (24/7 kid chats).
- **Headspace:** headspace.org.au (Mental health for 12-25).
- **Police:** 000 for emergencies; non-urgent 131 444.
- **Family Doctor:** For ongoing support.

**"If unsure, chat with Kids Helpline; better safe than sorry.**

# Shadow Banished: Step Into the Light

You've faced the dark side head-on, and you've made a top effort! By spotting red flags, reporting swiftly, recovering with care, and tapping resources, you're not just surviving; you're equipping your family to thrive. Remember, 80% of incidents resolve with proactive steps like yours; shadows can't stand the light of knowledge and support. You should feel empowered; you've turned potential bogeymen into banished myths. Now, carry that torch forward to sustain the wins in our final subject.

**"Light the shadows with action, you're the family's beacon!"**

**74% of kids encounter inappropriate content, but talks and tools help 80% navigate safely!**

# Elevating Your Game with Continuous Strategies and Resources

G'day, champions! With the dark side lit, it's time to lock in those wins for good.
So far, we've journeyed through the jungle, set up camp, modelled the way, chatted the chats, spotted snakes, pirate-proofed privacy, and lit the dark side.

Now we cement it all in place: Turning one-off actions into lifelong habits. Although this isn't the finish line for you, as online safety evolves like tech itself, with 82% of Australian parents requiring ongoing resources to keep up.

I'll give it my best shot to wrap things up by ensuring you're prepared for check-ins, challenges, directories, and a victory quiz.

# Regular Check-Ins and Updates: How to Keep Your Game Strong

I always wanted the book to be there whenever you need it, and what better way than to set up tools you can use for monthly check-ins to help keep on top of gaps early, with 75% of families avoiding slip-ups this way. So I tried to set up multiple ways for you to do so; then you can pick how many you feel like doing. But let's start with a quick look back to see where your head's at.

## Check-Ins Tips:

**Review Device Reports:** Screen time spikes? Adjust limits.
**Recall Check:** Verify if your iOS Downtime or Android Family Link settings are still blocking late-night scrolls, did you remember to test them last month? (Page 21)

**Update Apps/OS:** New features block fresh threats.
**Recall Check:** Scan for privacy pirates by updating apps like TikTok. Check if Family Pairing (your loot-sealing tool) is enabled and working. (Page 71)

**Chat Refresh:** "Anything new online?" Keep your eyes open.
**Recall Check:** Revisit an age-specific script (e.g., for tweens on strangers), quiz yourself: Did you log the last chat in your tracker, and what was the win? (Page 39)

**Tool Tune-Up:** Test controls; add new filters.
**Recall Check:** Ensure your media agreement rules (like no phones at dinner) are followed, and spot if your modelling habits from the self-quiz are slipping. (Page 33)

**Flag & Threat Scan:** Quick red flag review from The Dark Side or bullying signs. (Page 77)
**Recall Check:** "Seen any snake-like mean messages?", Use the Digital Jungle's family audit to rate current risks 1-5. (Page 14)

# Check-Ins Tips:

Turn check-ins into a visual victory board. Track monthly to see how far you've come, like levelling a character in a game. eSafety says monitored habits sustain safety for 85% of families; this tracker makes it easy without the fuss. You can add stickers for "boss level" months if you like!

Tracker Table Example (Can be designed however you like):

| Date | Controls Checked? | Habits Refreshed? | Chats Logged? |
|---|---|---|---|
| | ☐ | ☐ | ☐ |
| | ☐ | ☐ | ☐ |
| | ☐ | ☐ | ☐ |
| | ☐ | ☐ | ☐ |
| | ☐ | ☐ | ☐ |
| | ☐ | ☐ | ☐ |

> These recall checks reinforce the book's lessons without the hassle; we check in to keep our skills sharp.

## Wins/Notes

_______________

_______________

_______________

_______________

_______________

# 30-Day Challenge Calendar

One Small Task Daily for a Month
This is merely an example; ultimately, it's entirely up to you how you design your 30-day challenge. However, you might find this approach useful.
(Full Breakdown on Next Pages)

| | | | |
|---|---|---|---|
| | | 1 Password Power-Up | 2 Device Discovery |
| 6 Bullying Buster | 7 Random Inspection | 8 Screen Time Check | 9 Red Flag Scan |
| 13 Kindness Code | 14 Resource Bookmark | 15 Mid-Month Win | 16 Password Round 2 |
| 20 Dark Side Drill | 21 Pledge Update | 22 Screen Balance Day | 23 Scam Defence |
| 27 Full Audit Refresh | 28 Victory Prep | 29 Custom Challenge | 30 Grand Finale |

# Let's Build Habits Today!

| | | |
|---|---|---|
| 3 App Audit | 4 Role Model Reflection | 5 Quick Chat |
| 10 Scam Spotter Game | 11 Tool Tune-Up | 12 Family Zone Setup |
| 17 Chat Refresh | 18 App Privacy Boost | 19 Habit Mirror |
| 24 Zone Expansion | 25 Positive Post | 26 Resource Dive |

NOTES

2026

# Full 30-Day Breakdown

Feeling a bit overwhelmed by the 30-day challenge? That's totally normal; every journey starts with one small step! Remember, this isn't about ticking every single box perfectly; it's about gentle progress that builds real habits over time. Pick just 3–5 days to begin with, celebrate every win (even the tiny ones), and watch your family's confidence grow. You've already journeyed through the whole jungle; this is simply your victory lap. You've got this!

| Day | Challenge | Why it helps |
|---|---|---|
| 1 | Password Power-Up: Change one weak family password to a strong one (e.g., mix caps, numbers, symbols). | Weak passwords cause 90% of breaches; start strong to protect info from day one! |
| 2 | Device Discovery: List all family devices and rate risks 1-5 (1=safe, 5=dodgy). Discuss as a group. | Spots gaps early; 57% of parents miss this, leaving kids exposed. |
| 3 | App Audit: Pick 3 apps, check privacy settings (e.g., private mode on). | Reduces oversharing; proper settings block 70% of leaks. |
| 4 | Role Model Reflection: Note one bad habit (e.g., scrolling at dinner) and swap it for a good one today. | Kids mimic 70% of your behaviour, which helps to reduce risks. |

**Notes (Your Custom Tweaks/Results)**

| Day | Challenge | Why it helps |
|---|---|---|
| 5 | Quick Chat: Have a 2-min talk on "online strangers" using a Page 39 script. | Builds trust; early chats cut grooming by 50%. |
| 6 | Bullying Buster: Review one social app for block/report features, practise spotting mean comments. | 53% of kids face bullying; knowing tools resolves 70% of cases. |
| 7 | Random Inspection: Grab a device without your child's knowledge and go through the steps we discussed. | Helps to make sure children aren't disabling or keeping secrets from you. |
| 8 | Screen Time Check: Use device reports to see weekly usage, set one new limit. | Balances life; over 2 hours daily spikes addiction risks. |
| 9 | Red Flag Scan: Discuss Bullying Flags from Page 56 (e.g., secretive chats). | Early spotting cuts exploitation by 80%. |
| 10 | Scam Spotter Game: Play a quick true/false on common scams (use Page 69 examples). | Spots 80% fakes; 60% Aussies hit scams yearly. |
| 11 | Tool Tune-Up: Update one parental control app or filter. | Patches new threats; outdated tools miss 60% of junk. |

**Notes (Your Custom Tweaks/Results)**

| Day | Challenge | Why it helps |
| --- | --- | --- |
| 12 | Family Zone Setup: Create one new tech-free zone (e.g., bedrooms), test it tonight. | Boosts connections; reduces addiction by 50%. |
| 13 | Kindness Code: Share a positive online post as a family, discuss why it's good. | Models anti-bullying; positive habits cut conflicts by 60%. |
| 14 | Resource Bookmark: Save 2 sites from the directory (e.g., eSafety, Kids Helpline). | Quick access sustains safety for 85% of families. |
| 15 | Mid-Month Win: Celebrate progress, review ticks, high-five, add a fun offline activity. | Motivation matters; halfway boosts completion by 50%. |
| 16 | Password Round 2: Strengthen another account with 2FA. | Adds a moat; cuts hacks by 90%. |
| 17 | Chat Refresh: Redo a bullying role-play from page 60. | Reinforces; consistent talks help 80% bounce back. |
| 18 | App Privacy Boost: Toggle one more setting (e.g., location off in games). | Blocks tracking; 25% of kids harassed from leaks. |

| Notes (Your Custom Tweaks/Results) |
| --- |
| |

| Day | Challenge | Why it helps |
|---|---|---|
| 19 | Habit Mirror: Reflect on your scrolling, set a personal limit today. | Leads by example; mimics reduce your risks too! |
| 20 | Dark Side Drill: Quiz family on one red flag and response. | Preps for real; intervention heals 70% of cases. |
| 21 | Pledge Update: Tweak your privacy oath if needed, re-sign. | Keeps it fresh; accountability lasts longer. |
| 22 | Screen Balance Day: Track time, aim for under 2 hours of fun, swap excess with play. | Fights overuse; balance cuts mood issues by 50%. |
| 23 | Scam Defence: Discuss a news scam story, spot the tricks. | Real-world prep; awareness saves from 80% traps. |
| 24 | Zone Expansion: Add another tech-free spot (e.g., car rides). | Strengthens bonds; more zones mean less conflict. |
| 25 | Positive Post Challenge: Create and share a kind online message. | Builds anti-bullying culture; positivity spreads! |

| Notes (Your Custom Tweaks/Results) |
|---|
| |

| Day | Challenge | Why it helps |
|---|---|---|
| **26** | Resource Dive: Explore one bookmarked site, note a new tip. | Ongoing learning; 85% stay ahead with resources. |
| **27** | Full Audit Refresh: Re-rate devices/apps from Day 2, note improvements. | Tracks progress; spots new gaps early. |
| **28** | Victory Prep: Quiz the family on a highlighted part of the book and share a laugh over any previous mistakes. | Reinforces all; recaps boost retention by 50%. |
| **29** | Custom Challenge: Pick a weak spot from the month, tackle it today. | Personalises; ownership sustains habits. |
| **30** | Grand Finale: Review all ticks, celebrate big (e.g., family outing), plan next month's repeat. | Cements win; monthly cycles keep safety at 75% effectiveness. |

| Notes (Your Custom Tweaks/Results) |
|---|
| |

**This calendar cycles through the book's key areas (controls, habits, chats, etc.) for reinforcement. Feel free to tweak it for your family's age and needs. If printing, add space for stickers or drawings to keep it fun. You've got this; repeat quarterly for levelling up!**

# Emerging Threats Watchlist:

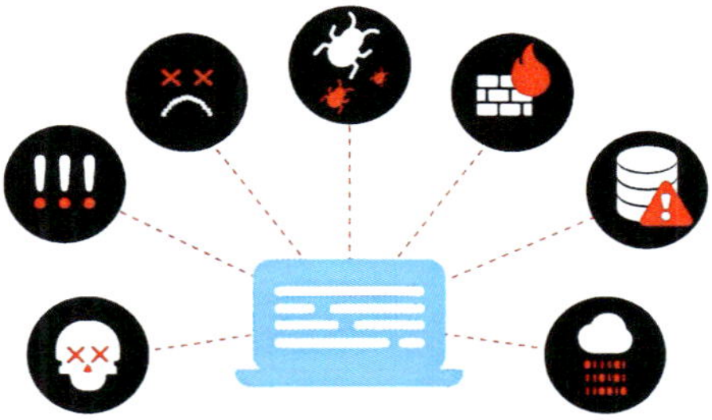

Tech will always move forwards, so trying to stay ahead can be tricky. Here's a list of rising trends to keep an eye on in 2026 and beyond:

| | |
|---|---|
| AI Deepfakes: Fake videos/audio tricking kids (e.g., "celebrity" scams). | Watch For: Odd messages; teach "verify with me." |
| VR/AR Worlds: Immersive games with stranger interactions. | Watch For: Overuse; set time limits and "real-world checks." |
| Data Broker Dangers: Apps selling kid info for targeted ads. | Watch For: Spam surges; opt out via privacy settings. |
| Crypto/Gaming Scams: "Earn Rewards" Lures in Games | Watch For: Money requests; ban in-app purchases |

**5 Quick Random Questions. Let's see where you are at now that you have finished the book!**

1. Set controls?____________________ (Yes/No)
2. Modelled habits?____________________ (Yes/No)
3. Had safety chats?____________________ (Yes/No)
4. Privacy pledged?____________________ (Yes/No)
5. Resources bookmarked?____________________ (Yes/No)

**SCORING:**

**5 YES:**________________ **Master Leveller!**

**3-4:**________________ **Strong Player.**

**1-2:**________________ **Rising Star.**

**0:**________ **New Game+, Restart Book.**

# Bonus Parental Tips

These are simple, low-effort ideas from real Aussie parents that don't take much time but can make a real difference. Pick one or two to try, with no pressure to do everything at once.

**The Safe Word System:** Agree on a special family safe word (like "pineapple" or "red light"). If your child says it during gaming, a video call, or anywhere really, it means "I feel uncomfortable or unsafe, please help me right now." Practise it together a couple of times so it feels natural. This gives kids an easy, shame-free way to get help without explaining everything on the spot.

**The Phone Check Agreement:** For older kids and teens, create a calm agreement: "I can ask to see your phone or laptop anytime, but I'll always explain why and we'll look at it together." This builds trust instead of secret checking and works especially well once they're 13+. Many families find it reduces arguments and sneaky behaviour.

**The Pause & Ask Rule:** Before posting, sharing a photo, or sending a message, teach your child to pause for three seconds and ask: "Would I say this to their face?" or "Would I be okay if Mum or Dad saw this?" It's a tiny habit that prevents many regrets and helps them think before they act.

**Device-Free Dinner:** Make one meal a day (usually dinner) completely device-free. No phones at the table, just conversation. It's one of the easiest ways to reconnect as a family and model healthy boundaries without feeling like a big rule.

**The One Question Rule:** At bedtime or during car rides, ask just one open question: "What was the best and trickiest thing that happened online today?" It keeps communication open without feeling like an interrogation and often leads to surprisingly honest answers.

Start with whichever feels easiest for your family. Small habits like these stack up over time and make a bigger difference than you might expect.

# Age specific Tips

Here are quick, practical tips tailored to different ages. Pick what feels right for your family and adjust as they grow.

**5–8 years (Little Ones)**

- Keep devices in common areas only, never in bedrooms.
- Use simple rules: "Ask Mum or Dad before sharing any photo or name."
- Turn on all built-in parental controls and Restricted Mode on YouTube.
- Make screen time a shared activity; sit with them and talk about what they see.
- Teach the Safe Word system early so they know how to get help immediately.

**9–12 years (Tweens)**

- Set clear time limits (e.g., 1 hour for games/social media) and stick to them together.
- Review privacy settings with them every few months; make it a team job.
- Use the "Pause & Ask" rule before posting: "Would I say this to their face?"
- Have weekly "What was the best and trickiest thing online this week?" chats.
- Check friend lists and group chats regularly; do it openly so it's not spying.

**13–16 years (Teens)**

- Shift to open-phone agreements instead of secret checks: "I can ask to see it, but I'll always explain why."
- Discuss real scenarios (deepfakes, sexting pressure, grooming) using scripts (Page 39).
- Encourage them to come to you first if something feels off; no punishment for honesty.
- Review app permissions together when they want a new app.
- Keep one tech-free zone or activity (e.g., dinner or Sunday mornings) to stay connected offline.

These are starting points; every child is different. The most powerful thing you can do is keep the conversations going with kindness and consistency.

# Resource Directory: Your Powerful Backup

Need more help on a particular topic that I didn't cover? Head over to one of the sites listed below for an even more detailed look at so many other topics. QR codes to make things easier!

**eSafety Commissioner: esafety.gov.au (Guides, reports).**

**Google Be Internet Awesome: beinternetawesome.withgoogle.com (Games, pledges).**

**Kids Helpline: kidshelpline.com.au 1800 55 1800 (Chats).**

# Victory Lap! Let's Celebrate!!

Champions, you've levelled up from jungle newbies to safety superstars, congrats on the epic journey! From spotting snakes to pirate-proofing, you've got the tools to lock in wins forever.

Remember, 75% sustain safety with these habits; you're not just surviving the digital wilds, you're thriving. Feel the power: Small steps like check-ins and challenges circle back to that first audit, building a resilient family fortress.

**"Level up life! Safety's your ultimate power-up!**

"You've walked through the digital jungle, faced the snakes, protected your family, and come out stronger. Now it's time to celebrate; your family's safe future starts now."

# You've Got This: Your Family's Safe Future Starts Now

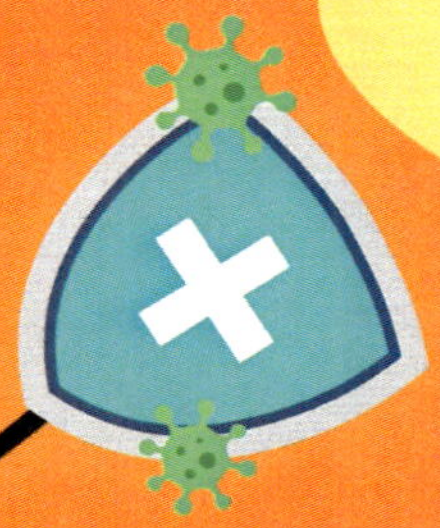

You did it. So what now...
Not many parents take the initiative like you have to enhance online safety. With your newfound knowledge, tools, and confidence, you're now better equipped to protect your family online, and you did it all the no-nonsense Aussie way.

This bonus section of the book serves as your victory lap. Let's celebrate what you've achieved, lock in your family plan, and look ahead together by giving you extra tools and resources to make sure that anything that comes your way, you can handle.

But before we celebrate, I've got a favour to ask you.

# GOT QUESTIONS?

Feel free to reach out by sending us an email at: support@nononsenseguide.com.au. We'd love to hear how this book has impacted your life!

# NONONSENSEGUIDE.COM.AU

# NO-NONSENSE GUIDE TO ONLINE SAFETY

Thank you, Thank you, Thank you!!

The no-nonsense guide to online safety has been one of my favourite but most challenging books I've created. The thought of it helping a single parent in need makes every single hour I put into this worth it.

I truly cannot thank you enough for purchasing this book, but I do need your help. Reviews in this world are powerful, and your review could be the difference between another parent deciding if they should purchase the book for themselves. So please leave a review and share on socials whatever you can do to help me on my mission of making sure parents around Australia regain the power to feel safe online again.

Check out our website if you would like to reach out to me with any questions or if you have an idea for the next no-nonsense guide, but until then, thank you once again for your support.

Have a great day and I'll see you in the next one.

-Nathan

# What You've Achieved

Take a moment to look back at how far you've come.

You started this journey feeling overwhelmed by the risks and not knowing where to begin. Today, you know how to spot risks early and protect your kids without turning into the fun police. You've learned to set up strong device controls and privacy settings on iOS and Android that actually work for your family, no more guessing or hoping for the best.

You've become a true role model for your kids and know how to model the behaviour you want to see and have calm, effective conversations that build real trust instead of fear or arguments.

You can now recognise bullying, grooming, and inappropriate content, and respond quickly and confidently when it happens. Most powerfully of all, you now know how to handle the hardest situation: when your own child is the one causing harm. You have the tools to guide them with accountability and love, without shame or blame.

You've also learned how to keep safety going long-term with regular check-ins, challenges, and the right resources at your fingertips.

Most importantly, you've learned that online safety isn't about living in fear or trying to be the perfect parent. It's about consistent, loving guidance, and you're already doing it.

You should feel incredibly proud of yourself. This isn't just a book you read. It's a journey you completed. Your family is safer, stronger, and more connected because of the work you've put in.

You've got this.

# Proud Moments & Wins

Let's celebrate your wins, big and small.

**What are you most proud of learning from this journey?**

1. ______________________________

2. ______________________________

3. ______________________________

**What I've Learned About My Family:**

______________________________

______________________________

**One Thing I'll Keep Doing:**

______________________________

______________________________

**One Thing I'm Letting Go Of**

______________________________

______________________________

You've experienced growth, and so has your family. Each small step you've taken has made a significant impact.
Return to this page whenever you feel overwhelmed by technology, as a reminder of how you faced challenges before and triumphed, and know that you can do it again!

Keep going!!!

# Safety Signal Cards

**As a bonus, I wanted to talk about a secret weapon for parents to use when words are hard in certain situations.**

If you bought the Starter Pack, you'll already have your set of 16 Safety Signal Cards tucked inside. If not, you can still purchase them on our website, where I explain them in more detail, but let me explain the basics of how they work.

These little cards are one of the simplest ideas in the whole book, but they work brilliantly. Some kids freeze when something online upsets, scares, or makes them uncomfortable. They know they should tell you, but the words get stuck, or because of the new rules you've introduced over the course of this book, they might not know how to approach you themselves. The cards give them an easy, private way to say "I need help" without having to explain everything on the spot.

Think of them as a bridge. They turn a scary or awkward moment into a simple handover that says, "I trust you enough to tell you... but not in front of everyone."

This builds trust that they can come to you when things happen, but it also gives you the time to study by going straight to the part of the book you need, as they are all colour-coded to match the specific part of the book needed for the card given to you.

### How to introduce them to your kids

Sit down as a family or individually one night and say something like: "Hey, we've got these special cards now. If something online ever makes you feel weird, worried, or just plain yuck, you don't have to explain straight away. Just grab the card you need and hand it to Mum or Dad, and we will come to see you when you're ready."

**Make it normal.** Keep the cards somewhere easy to access (bedroom drawer, kitchen bench, fridge). The more boring and everyday they feel, the more likely your child will actually use them.

## Simple Rules

**Any card handed over = stop what you're doing and listen. No phones, no "just a sec."**

**You don't have to explain straight away. The card is enough to start the conversation.**

**No punishment for using a card. Ever. This is a safe signal, not a dobbing system.**

**Parent's job is to stay calm, thank them for trusting you, and ask "What do you need right now?" (a hug, a chat, help blocking someone, etc.)**

## Real examples of when a card might get used

- Your child hands you the "I made a mistake online" card after they accidentally sent something they regret or clicked on something they shouldn't have.
- Your daughter quietly gives you the "I saw something that upset me" card after coming across a video or message that scared or worried her.
- Your son slides you the "Someone is being mean to me online" card because a group chat has turned nasty and he doesn't know what to do.

**When they use one, you've already won. They are choosing to reach out instead of suffering in silence. These cards aren't magic, but they remove the biggest barrier, the horrible moment of thinking "how do I even start this conversation?" If you don't have the physical set yet and you'd like one, head to nononsenseguide.com.au and pick them up today. So your kids have a simple way to tell you when they need you most.**

# Family Audit Checklist: Quick Self-Assessment Tool Extra Pages

| App | Risk | Screen Time | Ask the Child What they have seen lately? (Recomended Videos) |
|---|---|---|---|
| | | | |
| | | | |
| | | | |
| | | | |
| | | | |
| | | | |
| | | | |
| | | | |
| | | | |
| | | | |
| | | | |
| | | | |
| | | | |
| | | | |
| | | | |
| | | | |
| | | | |

# Family Audit Checklist: Quick Self-Assessment Tool Extra Pages

| App | Risk | Screen Time | Ask the Child What they have seen lately? (Recomended Videos) |
|---|---|---|---|
| | | | |
| | | | |
| | | | |
| | | | |
| | | | |
| | | | |
| | | | |
| | | | |
| | | | |
| | | | |
| | | | |
| | | | |
| | | | |
| | | | |
| | | | |
| | | | |
| | | | |

# Extra Agreement Template:

## Family Agreement

I, ..............................., the Kid/parent of ............................, have read and reviewed the Family Agreement for the Rules and Regulations for the device I'm about to receive. I acknowledge and agree to the following:

**Child Signature**

Name:______________________

Signature:______________________

Date: ______________________

**Adult Signature**

Name:______________________

Signature:______________________

Date: ______________________

## Extra Agreement Template:

# Family Agreement

I, ..............................., the Kid/parent of ..............................., have read and reviewed the Family Agreement for the Rules and Regulations for the device I'm about to receive. I acknowledge and agree to the following:

**Child Signature**

Name:______________________

Signature:______________________

Date: ______________________

**Adult Signature**

Name:______________________

Signature:______________________

Date: ______________________

# Extra Agreement Template:

## Family Agreement

I, ................................, the Kid/parent of ............................., have read and reviewed the Family Agreement for the Rules and Regulations for the device I'm about to receive. I acknowledge and agree to the following:

**Child Signature**

Name:____________________

Signature:____________________

Date: ____________________

**Adult Signature**

Name:____________________

Signature:____________________

Date: ____________________

# Extra Agreement Template:

## Family Agreement

I, ................................, the Kid/parent of .............................., have read and reviewed the Family Agreement for the Rules and Regulations for the device I'm about to receive. I acknowledge and agree to the following:

**Child Signature**

Name:____________________

Signature:____________________

Date: ____________________

**Adult Signature**

Name:____________________

Signature:____________________

Date: ____________________

# Notes

# Notes

# Notes

# Notes

# Notes

# Sources & Further Reading

All statistics and guidance in this book are drawn from current public resources (primarily the eSafety Commissioner, licensed under CC BY 4.0 where applicable) and updated as of 2026. Always check the latest information directly from official sources, as online safety evolves quickly.

**Official Australian Resources**

- eSafety Commissioner – esafety.gov.au | 1800 880 176
- Kids Helpline – kidshelpline.com.au | 1800 55 1800
- Parentline – 1300 30 1300
- Beyond Blue – beyondblue.org.au | 1300 22 4636

**Helpful Tools & Websites**

- Google Be Internet Awesome – beinternetawesome.withgoogle.com
- NetSmartz – netsmartz.org
- ThinkUKnow Australia – thinkuknow.org.au

**Books for Further Reading**

- The Whole-Brain Child – Daniel J. Siegel
- Screenwise – Devorah Heitner

**Once again thankyou for checking this out!!**

Made in United States
North Haven, CT
05 November 2026

21766153R60066